The Kuwento Book

**AN ANTHOLOGY OF
FILIPINO STORIES + POEMS**

The Kuwento Book

AN ANTHOLOGY OF FILIPINO STORIES + POEMS

Edited by **Pat Lindsay C. Catalla-Buscaino**

Foreword by Jenah Maravilla

Contributing Authors

Al Aguilar		Noureliza Montifar
Anthony Pabillano	Genesis Lingling	Royal Sumikat
Chezka Laddaran	Holly Lim	Rudy Jr. Calera
Christy Panis Poisot	Jacob Magallanes	Sheralynn Magallanes
Cybil Joy Pallugna-Saenz	Jay Menes	Sophia Emille
Dustin Domingo	Jermuel P. Manarin	Tiffany Sloan
Florencio Guinhawa	Krystelle Robeniol	Trisha Morales
G. Chris Villanasco	Krystle Tugadi	Victor Barnuevo Velasco
Gabbie Aquino-Adriatico	Marie Salazar	Zoe Gapayao

TEXAS

Copyright © 2023 by Kuwento Co. LLC

All rights reserved. No part of this publication may be reproduced, stored or transmitted in any form or by any means, electronic, mechanical, photocopying, recording, scanning, or otherwise without written permission from the publisher. It is illegal to copy this book, post it to a website, or distribute it by any other means without written permission from the publisher or author, except as permitted by U.S. copyright law.

The stories and poems are entirely from the perception and point of view of each contributing author. Any names, character, beliefs, ideologies, and incidents portrayed in it are the work of the contributing author and are not a direct reflection or embodiment of Kuwento Co. LLC beliefs or ideologies.

Cover designed by Kuwento Co.

First Paperback Edition, 2023 | Paperback ISBN: 979-8-9865457-6-9

First Hardcover Edition, 2023 | Hardback ISBN: 979-8-9865457-8-3

First E-Book Edition, 2023 | E-Book ISBN: 979-8-9865457-7-6

Library of Congress Control Number: 2023932031

www.KuwentoCo.com
info@kuwentoco.com
@KuwentoCo

To all aspiring writers, dreamers, storytellers, and cultural bearers—you are the author of your life stories.

To Raymar da Star—keep on dancing

Contents

Foreword   1
JENAH MARAVILLA

1. Introduction   3
   PAT LINDAY "PINKY" C. CATALLA-BUSCAINO

2. Press Release   8
   KRYSTELLE ROBENIOL

3. Born In Silence   10
   TIFFANY SLOAN

4. I Cannot Speak My Mind   15
   CHRISTY PANIS POISOT

5. Be(longing)   21
   HOLLY LIM

6. Our Heavy Doors — 25
   KRYSTLE TUGADI

7. Trip To Manila: A Poetry Collection — 32
   JACOB MAGALLANES

8. Losing Lola — 34
   G. CHRIS VILLANASCO

9. Death By A Broken Heart — 41
   GABBIE AQUINO-ADRIATICO

10. My Ancestor, From The Great Beyond — 45
    ROYAL SUMIKAT

11. Dear Inay — 58
    CYBIL JOY PALLUGNA-SAENZ

12. Mommy's Kuwento — 64
    NOURELIZA MONTIFAR

13. Huwag Buksan Ang Pinto — 70
    JERMUEL P. MANARIN

14. Am I An Introvert? — 73
    DUSTIN DOMINGO

15. My Own Privilege — 78
    TRISHA MORALES

16. Bangon — 81
    CHEZKA LADDARAN

17. Pay It Forward   89
FLORENCIO GUINHAWA

18. Parol   96
GENESIS LINGLING

19. Mangarap Ka   108
CHEZKA LADDARAN

20. Never Heard Of Such A Thing: How I Became An International Storyteller   112
JAY MENES

21. A Personal Statement   121
MARIE SALAZAR

22. balikbayan box   127
AL AGUILAR

23. Mapping Love and Longing in Chicago   129
VICTOR BARNUEVO VELASCO

24. Plastic   136
DUSTIN DOMINGO

25. August, 2000   137
SOPHIA EMILLE

26. Thanksgiving Day   139
ANTHONY TUGADE PABILLANO

27.	A Gaysian Friendsgiving DUSTIN DOMINGO	143
28.	The Last Feather RUDY JR. CALERA	147
29.	Motherland TIFFANY SLOAN	153
30.	New Moon Peaches SHERALYNN MAGALLANES	154
31.	On Performance TIFFANY SLOAN	158
32.	Salamat Houston GABBIE AQUINO-ADRIATICO	160
33.	Uwi Na Tayo ZOE GAPAYAO	165
34.	The Land Loves Us Back SHERALYNN MAGALLANES	168

Reflection Questions	171
Acknowledgements	173
About the Contributing Authors	175
About the Editor	231

Foreword

JENAH MARAVILLA

One thing you must know about me, dear Reader, is that I am a sucker for a good story. At 9 years old, I already had a reputation as a bookworm, with my nose buried in a different book at every family function. That Christmas, I was gifted *Chicken Soup for the Kid's Soul*, an anthology much like this, filled with real-life anecdotes that made me believe in the magic of the ordinary. As a child, these stories were not afraid to evoke deep and truthful emotions within me.

These vicarious and visceral experiences are the seeds of my art-making and nonprofit work. In co-authoring *Filipinos in Houston* with Christy Poisot, my eyes opened to the vibrancy of our community's lives. These bright bits of history and hero-making moments couldn't all fit into a photo-heavy publication, and after having the pleasure of reading through *The Kuwento Book*, I am ecstatic to know that stories like the ones I've encountered have a home. I am reminded of my once-beloved *Chicken Soup for the Kid's Soul*, but the difference now is that this is uniquely *ours*. (*Sinigang for the Pilipino Soul*, if you will.) I truly hope this book gets into the hands of other eager bookworms, big and small.

Through nonprofit work, I met the formidable, bubbly, and inspiring Dr. Pat Lindsay Catalla-Buscaino, (affectionately known as Ate Pinky). From the start, I knew her voice was powerful, and she had something to say. I did not yet know the power she could instill within *others* to make them understand that *they* had something to say—until I had the honor of witnessing Ate Pinky's Doctoral Defense a few years back. I left the room teary-eyed, fully feeling the weight of her work. A natural orator, she had the room hanging onto her every word as she recanted the stories of Filipino American students navigating higher education. It was the first time I had felt seen in the struggle of being first generation Filipino American.

One thing you must know about Ate Pinky, dear Reader, is that she sees all things through. Not just left in the annals of the Ivory Tower, the stories she had carried, now carry her—manifesting into this lovely collection of our community's short stories, prose, and poetry; I am delighted to be part of its introduction. Psychologist Carl R. Rogers once said, "What is most personal, is most universal." And that rings true for this and everything that Ate Pinky touches.

Ingat lagi,

Jenah Maravilla

1

Introduction

PAT LINDAY "PINKY" C. CATALLA-BUSCAINO

For every worthwhile endeavor, comes a journey.

The creation of this anthology began in the early pandemic days of 2020. I was hankering to do something creative and I had been wanting to make a book. Not just any book, but one that reflected the stories of my community. With this new endeavor, I was determined to collect *kuwentos* and create a collection of stories by Filipino Americans. I put out a call for submissions, posted it on my personal Facebook, and surprisingly, people responded with enthusiasm. Submissions started coming in, and I was excited but also nervous. As the pandemic progressed, the project was at a stand still and I had to re-evaluate my circumstances.

As the saying goes, life happens, and it happened real hard. I know many people experienced extreme loss during this time, bringing out the essence of our humanity. I had the biggest loss of my life occur on

May 22, 2022, when my best friend, Raymar G. Resuello, suddenly passed away at the young age of 37. Raymar was a bright light in my life and he was the brother I never had. He was the life of every party, he knew the coolest dessert spots in L.A., he always wore the trendiest outfits, and he bought me and my sister clothes from Forever 21 to be trendy just like him. In the last couple of years of his life, we would always share stories of our childhood growing up in Culver City, Los Angeles. Raymar and I were classmates since kindergarten, and we were fortunate to be surrounded by a diverse cohort of schoolmates, many of whom were Filipina/x/o.

We had a lot in common. For starters, both our moms worked together at the same hospital before we were born. We were both the *ate* and *kuya*, eldest, of the family, with younger siblings, Kristian and Christine Mae, who were also classmates and just days apart in birthdays. We were both Leos, and specifically "1984 Olympic babies," as Raymar would recall. We both loved the performing arts and participating in school musicals. Lastly, we both LOVED Filipino movies and variety TV shows featuring our favorite Filipino boy bands and love teams—solidifying our best friendship in the summer of 1997.

During our many long talks, we shared our perspectives of Filipina/x/o identity, culture, family, education, career, politics, and faith. I was so lucky to be able to unpack those conversations with Raymar, someone who understood what I went through. Whenever I couldn't remember a person or memory from our past, I would immediately call Raymar and ask him. Of course, he knew the answers and recalled every detail of the memory. Raymar was my *kuwento keeper*. I had grown dependent on him as my life historian. He was there for every important moment in my life. Like being my debut partner when I turned 18. Taking me to prom and winning the crown together. Or the time he made a surprise visit to Texas to attend my doctorate graduation. He helped me pick out my wedding dress, and when I got married, he was the first one to give me a hug while crying his eyes out. I never thought my childhood best friend of 25 years wouldn't be here to grow old with me, and I with him. I dedicate this book to Raymar because he continues to inspire me to keep going and to keep the stories alive.

Fast forward to October 2022. I was in a better position to create the anthology book. I needed to fill the emptiness, numbness, and emotional exhaustion of Raymar's loss with something meaningful. This time around, I decided to make the *kuwento* process a community challenge to create a Filipino anthology book as part of National Write a Novel / Memoir Month in November. Once again, I put out a call for submissions, and this time I promised to see it through. I hosted weekly writing and storytelling workshops to help people craft their stories in the safety of other aspiring writers. Several participants who attended those workshops have also contributed to this anthology—*salamat* shout out to Jay, Christy, Cybil, Trisha, Sheralynn, Holly, Krystelle, Anthony, Al, Tito Flor, and Gabbie.

The Kuwento Book: An Anthology of Filipino Stories + Poems is a beautiful mixture of original *kuwento*s from all over the world. You will read stories that resonate with you and will pull your heart strings. You will read a piece and completely understand the author's perspective as if it were your own. There might also be *kuwentos* that challenge your opinions, making you reflect on your own beliefs. There are some tough, hard, and heartbreaking stories that contemplate on life, death, and the in-between—mirroring the times we are living through.

As a independent publisher, I have made a conscious decision to make sure the voice of each contributing author is heard in their own voice and language. Aspiring writers—even seasoned writers—get hung up on the perfection of writing, because we have grown up with so many literary rules. Proper grammar is important for many things, such as standardization, research writing, and clarity in perspective—but in Kuwento Co., it is not detrimental to the essence of a *kuwento*. Instead, I encourage writers to write what they want to say because readers want to hear the real you. Every time I say this, writers are immediately relieved, giving themselves permission to be raw, authentic, unabashed, and liberated from limitations.

As a body of work, *The Kuwento Book* is a dynamic and complex story of our people. I am proud to showcase the diversity of the contributing author's backgrounds, experiences, locations, and bilingual tongues—because this is what makes up the Filipina/x/o diaspora. Each *kuwento*, each poem, shines a light on a special aspect of our experience, revealing who we truly are as *kapwa*, one with+in each other.

I hope you enjoy reading, exploring, and unpacking the *kuwentos* of this book with yourself and with others. There are reflection questions at the end of the book to help you start dialoging about your thoughts with each other, just as I was able to talk with Raymar. If you are moved and inspired, I invite you to share your *kuwento* for the next anthology.

Raymar Resuello during his surprise visit to Houston, Texas in May 2019.

2

Press Release

KRYSTELLE ROBENIOL

WE ALL HAVE STORIES to tell, but we withhold them.
Perhaps to deny how we have been changed,
Or maybe for fear of being
misunderstood, measured, compared against.
Perhaps we withhold our story to *protect* those we love,
Because we fear they cannot hold it with us
Or perhaps because we feel *unworthy* of being held.

We may withhold to protect ourselves from the reliving.
From the pain or embarrassment that comes with these memories.

Perhaps you are accustomed
to keeping your problems to yourself,
For you have been raised to do so and now tell your daughters to do the same.

But despite what you have taught me—
my nature is to share these stories.
Not to bring shame, but to own my life.
To own my growth.
To connect to my community.

To know that I am not alone.
To know that I am worthy of love and acceptance
for everything I am
And everything I have been through.

And as I become a fuller person, I hope to empower you
To tell yours without shame.

3

Born In Silence

TIFFANY SLOAN

LAGANGILANG, ABRA, PHILIPPINES
MAY 1942, *The Japanese Occupation of the Philippines*

The air hung on the hillside, as if the forest was holding its breath in anticipation. With a rag clenched between her teeth, Nanang labored. Gun fire in the distance masked the struggle that took place in the secluded forest hut. She worked for a new life, fighting soundlessly for her unborn daughter while concealing the location of her small family. It was this moment that first welcomed Monica Jorque into the upturned world. Hushed prayers swaddled the newborn as Tatang, the congregation of one, leaned in to praise the miracle that made no noise.

THE JAPANESE INVASION OF Lagangilang was watched by the midday sun. Word of approaching soldiers prompted a local evacuation, sending Filipinos from their homes and into the surrounding landscape of agricultural fields and dense forests. Tatang, my great grandfather, hastily ushered his wife and two toddlers, Roming and Bopeep, from their bamboo dwelling. He'd gathered pots, pans, anything he could hold, knowing that his remaining wealth was cradled between his arms. His family was much farther downhill, moving toward the stream whose steep banks bordered their safety.

Nanang, my great grandmother, struggled to keep her footing. With Bopeep on her hip, and Roming's hand in hers, she led her children across the rocky bank. Bopeep, only freshly 2 years old, cried as she left everything she knew. The sounds of her loss were met with reprimands from her brother, wiser at 5 years old.

"Shhhhh! Bopeep, you're making too much noise!" The little girl could only cry in response, "Nanang, can we just leave her?"

"Tsk, *anak*, stay quiet."

Nanang continued to usher the bickering children across the river, but her footfalls slowed as she doubled over in pain. Bopeep cried louder, "Nanang! What's happening?"

"Stay quiet," Nanang dropped Roming's hand, "Roming, take your sister."

"Nanang—"

"Take her and go ahead. Stay together, we'll find you." Both children cried heavy tears as they moved across the stream and into the forest. They looked back as Nanang cautioned a step, only to be met with another surge of pain. She doubled over again, recognizing these surges as contractions. By this time, Tatang was at a full sprint in her direction and the children had disappeared between the trees. In May of 1942, Nanang was *very* pregnant, and her third child was about to join her in a struggle for survival.

Their survival strategy was silence.

Twenty miles away in the provincial capital, Father Gabriel held mass. A devout Catholic, my great uncle frequently administered services to the community, tending to the volume of prayers which needed to be received during occupation. He was unaware that in a make-shift hut in the forest of Lagangilang he had a new niece, waiting to be blessed. The pews of his cathedral were filled, and the songs of praise reverberated from the vaulted ceilings, enough faith for heaven to hear. On this day, the Japanese forces advanced rapidly, using aircraft to bomb significant structures across the northern Philippines. Father Gabriel's cathedral wouldn't hold another congregation, as he left this upturned world on the same day his niece entered it.

The news would reach Lagangilang through hushed whispers and soft-spoken prayers. When silence wasn't survival, silence was grief.

THE SECOND GENERATION'S MEMORY was disrupted by the static of time: *Japan, evacuate, hillside, labor, lola— silence.* I busied myself by browsing the shelves of the local library, hoping to find a text to fill the liminal space between these musings. Stooping down for a better view of the bottom shelves, I'm reminded of Sundays spent kneeling in prayer. If this library is my church, then this shelf has become my rosary— each volume of history a bead to count in prayer. I find myself perpetually drawn to this place of worship, my own site of silence.

The fragmented oral history passed down to me was a violent remembering. To me, sitting among these books was a ritual of reclamation, looking to the white authors to teach me of the culture my mother had left on the opposite side of the Pacific. The only half story I could stitch together was a memory of Nanang, but I couldn't place which generation she came from or the young *titas* and *titos* who had evacuated with her. Instead, I made a habit of collecting passages about my heritage and using them to rebuild my identity.

My recognition of the Filipinx estrangement with history began to trouble me. I thought that if I knew the dates of occupation, the strategies of invasion, and the responses of Filipinos on the ground, then I knew our culture. I knew our history. I knew our story. I had gathered every anthology I could hold and considered myself wealthy with knowledge. I thought reclaiming and remembering our collective past could be done without noise, but I came to realize that intergenerational understanding would never be found between white pages.

I call my *lola* and my *titas,* and these women begin the process of reflection: *Japan, evacuate, hillside, labor, lola—silence.*

"Did you know I had a nickname growing up, *anak?*" It's the middle of the night and she'd spent a long day gardening in her sun-drenched backyard, but *lola* eagerly revisited the past with me. "Everyone in the Philippines used to call me *baquita!*" She erupts into laughter and I join her as if I'm in on the joke, "They'd call me *baquita, kitang,* or *kits* for short! Do you know what that means, *anak? Baquita?* It's the Ilocano word for evacuate."

This is a woman who was born in silence, but her laughter has always made such a full and joyful noise. I pay respect to the survival strategy which kept my family alive, but the stories my family forged in strength, the oral histories which were forgotten when the second generation stopped listening, could no longer survive in silence.

4

I Cannot Speak My Mind

CHRISTY PANIS POISOT

I cannot speak my mind
My mouth in bind
My voice quieted

I could not hear the sound
No book to bound
History not told

I knew no heroes brown
No sheroes found
No Role model could it be

What was the scar
We carried from afar
That became the DNA me

Can we recant
The story around the fire
Sacrificed for that future desire?

To survive aggression
My smiling depression
My resting bitch face

Can you taste the ice,
Of the of that artic device
That paralyzed our civilization?

When tattoos glistened
Skin storied listened
Beautiful and brown

My words come from deep
Where we are asleep
Flowing to teach you

Its origin unknown
Fermented and sown
In the ground of our immigration

My heart pours
And spirit soars
Looking for a place to land

Did you not know
Friend or foe
The dance and final stand?

Poor and tired
The island acquired
The edge of the earth ENTRENCHED

We anchor back
Where we surfed the ocean
Angry happy DRENCHED

It was the sky above
We all looked with love
We dreamed of the return

I CANNOT SPEAK MY MIND

Land ancestors owned
Abandoned and screams
Only to see it burn

To that place it seems
Conquerors called the Philippines
Always waiting our turn

It is time to come home
From the place that we roam
Travelers, we may be

Generations American
Identity lost
Whitewashed as far as the eye can see

Two countries locked
In destinies embrace
One version erased

Still we bloom
Where we are planted
With the stars in our heart

Longing to connect
With family dispersed
Universes far apart

Languages lost
At tribalism cost
United we are not

We blend and burn
Our skin return
Identities are sought

In your child's eyes
What color do they see?
Will they know their family tree?

Are the branches twisted
with nooses or leaves?
artistic stories?

or stolen by thieves?
and still the widow grieves
Gold, God, and Glory

Kapwa is preached
But few are reached
Trying to eat.

Crab mentality reigns
For individual gains
Still tsinelas on your feet

Hope glimmer still
At the artist will
Best storytellers on the planet

One step forward
Two steps back
Can't you see, god damnit?

All are leaders,
None will follow,
The truth, sometimes hard to swallow.

Glimmer light
To my delight shows
In artist hallow

Once united for a cause
A force to be reckoned
Only then ancestors appear when beckoned

Let us name them
Tattoos not on pages
But on the color of our skin

I CANNOT SPEAK MY MIND

The meaning of Kapwa
No degrees of separation
We are all in the end just kin.

America is in the heart,
Brown Skin White Minds,
Enlightenment that grinds.

History - tsismis with footnotes told
Dawn Mabalon, know her name
She .... Made the story UNFOLD

The young can learn these treasures
No need to wait for Ph.Ds
Or lofty measures

Like a fingerprint or snowflake
Nobody can take
Your story is your own

From Stockton
To Houston, Chicago, New York
Quit your moan and groan

Look within and around
There, our narrative is found
Give it an honorable place

I beseech you create
Dig deep
It is written on your face

The anger, the love,
Fortunes, misfortunes made
The brilliance not to be played

The most beautiful in this room
Creative civilization
Are beyond colonization

Rather than disappear
We are evolved
Yet not resolved

Write it down
Manifest in Song
Why it is we long

Scenes engrained dreams
Visualize narrative, Paint
No colors for the faint

Moving as the ancients
Sultry Dance,
Make us trance

Stone, hammer, nail
Landscape willed
By the man who will build

Baybayin Tattoo
Language lost
Time to redeem the cost

The time has come
Slowly conquer fear
The Renaissance IS HERE

5

Be(longing)

HOLLY LIM

For a good part of my life, I longed to belong. And this might be an unpopular opinion, but nowadays, I find comfort in not belonging.

Since I stepped foot into this country, I have never felt like I 100% belonged. I was a small child when my mom and I arrived at LAX from the Philippines. We were picked up by relatives, and on the car ride to wherever home might be, I asked, "When will my eyes turn blue and my hair turn blonde?" The adults had a good hearty laugh at my kids-will-say-the-darnedest thing inquiry. Looking back, I wish an adult had told me that brown skin, dark brown eyes, and the darkest curly black hair are what we have, what we always will have, and that we are important and valuable as we are. Sometimes, elders unknowingly pass down curses to the next generation, but we all have the magic to break them. This is me breaking the curse.

Like many Filipino Americans, I *tried so hard* and even *dived* for any opportunity to blend in, be accepted, and be American. But that also meant hiding, deserting, and not liking parts of myself. I didn't like the ridicule and embarrassment that came from standing out. To be different meant getting hurt. By the second grade, there were enough incidents at recess of kids outright saying my snacks were weird. It got to the point where I hid in the bathroom during recess if I had Filipino snacks – it could be a *siopao*, an *ensaymada*, or my favorite – a sandwich filled with sliced bright, red, Purefoods hot dogs. If I could, I would've eaten that radioactive looking hot dog on a stick adorned with colorful marshmallows, happily waving it around and doing happy wiggles, like I did during my birthday parties in the Philippines. But that joy needed to be hidden away, and that's how it was for a while. That was the cost of trying to belong.

When Asian American and Pacific Islander (AAPI) hate and violence gained media attention during the COVID-19 pandemic, I began to see lots of Asian Americans claim they are "American" or "I was born here." That prompted lots of questions for me about belonging:

Does belonging require abandonment?

What does it mean to belong?

Where do Filipino/a/x Americans belong in a country that, in my opinion, has never wanted us except for our labor?

Where do I belong?

Does any of this even matter?

In a *New York Times* op-ed, Viet Thanh Nguyen wrote that, "Belonging will get us only so far, for belonging always involves exclusion." I agreed, and a light bulb went off. I realized that for marginalized communities, belonging is preached as the ultimate goal. Now, I question that. For me, I now see that belonging requires acceptance by anyone who embodies whiteness, and when that acceptance happens, practicing white supremacist culture at some level is required, like being okay with anti-blackness. Ultimately, belonging to the majority or mainstream requires the newly included to also exclude. Is this why when violence is inflicted on AAPI bodies, some say "I'm an American" to show their humanity, and therefore, their worthiness? What is the cost then, of the humanity of Asians who can't claim Americanness and whiteness?

Some Filipino/a/x American groups unknowingly participate in exclusion too, even when they mean to be inclusive. I'm looking at you, Friendship Games, and some of the current hip Pinay-curated spaces that emphatically exclaim "YOU BELONG HERE!" in their social media posts, but I surely don't feel like it when I am at their events. Because sometimes belonging to a Fil-Am org, group, and even families requires a performance. Sometimes at Filipino/a/x gatherings, I've noticed people share what degrees they've earned, the leadership or professional titles they've taken on, their salaries, talents, achievements, coolness, and whatever else people say or do to measure self-perceived worth. I wonder what these people would say if they were asked, "Who are you without the titles, roles, achievements, and talents? What is your essence? Most have difficulty answering who they really are without external qualifiers. Sometimes, the price of belonging is ourselves.

I now refuse to be sacrificed on the altar of other people's ideas of success, worthiness, and what is deemed respectable. I've learned which groups and spaces require me to abandon myself in order to be included, and I am now mindful about the friendships, relationships, and groups I chose to be a part of. I have also felt most at home not belonging anywhere, to anyone, or to anything – not this country, schools, organizations, at work, and even with some family members. That doesn't mean that I accept disrespect and oppressive treatment from others on any level. But to break this curse, I have to believe that I belong to myself, and that's more than enough.

6

Our Heavy Doors

KRYSTLE TUGADI

"I shouldn't have to be here," the Little Girl thought as the practice sight word "run" stared at her through the boxy television. She never thought watching television would boil up such resentment. How could this be? TV meant entertainment. But this? This wasn't it. Also, how was this room always so frigid? Was there no warmth on this side of the school?

Just months ago, the Little Girl was exhilarated when she discovered that putting letters together made words, and words made sentences. Her Lola, a retired elementary school teacher from the Philippines, carved out hours of their days together, recognizing and understanding the alphabet together through books and puzzles. Making sure the Little Girl still had a sense of her Filipino culture, her Lola would also teach her fun folk songs in Ilocano, their mother tongue, but learning how to read and speak in English always came first. The Little Girl would not realize the urgency of knowing the English language as a Filipina girl living in Southern California at four years old, nor would she grasp the weight her brown skin would have to carry later down the line. All she knew, in these most treasured moments, was that she loved spending time with her Lola and knowing that everything her Lola was passing down to her was becoming a part of her.

One Saturday afternoon after lunch, the Little Girl felt a slight jolt in her body directing her to her small library of children's books in her mother's room. She pulled out one of her favorites that her Lola would read to her. Her small fingers paged through a first-edition Charlie Brown All-Stars Book. She stopped at a random page and placed her pointer finger at a random word. The Little Girl looked at the first letter and sounded it out. "Ffffff..." she began, ".....iiiiinuuuuhhhhhdddduh...fiiiinnduh...FIND!" An intense rush zapped through her body! She felt electric. She felt unstoppable. The Little Girl felt like she solved the ultimate puzzle of life. She kept going. She put her finger on the next word, and the next, and the next. The Little Girl could barely contain herself and ran to her Lola, showing her newfound discovery. "Lola, Lola! I can read! I can read!" She read the words she could string together, and her Lola took her in her arms and said, *"Dayta ti apok!"* meaning, "That's my granddaughter!" in Ilocano. The Little Girl's Lola was full of joy seeing how their time together had manifested into this empowering moment for her granddaughter. Reading at such a young age also meant that her granddaughter could get a real head start in this foreign country. The hope that her granddaughter could have all the opportunities promised in this country made this move all worth it. Together they sang *Dua Bilit*, the Little Girl's favorite Ilocano folk song, to celebrate this moment.

Months after this literary epiphany, the Little Girl walked to her first kindergarten class with her head held high and excited for all the scholastic adventures that awaited her. Her new school was right down the street from her house, so she didn't feel too far away from her Lola. On her first day of class, the Little Girl's Mom and Lola accompanied her. When they got to school, the Little Girl reached up on her tippy toes and put her tiny hand on the doorknob with the feeling that this was the beginning of the rest of her life. She turned the door handle and pulled the tall maroon-colored door. But the door was very heavy, and she could barely open it. Her Lola saw her struggle and helped her eager granddaughter. The fact that this door was this heavy to open, alarmed the little girl. How would she open the door if her Lola wasn't there? She shrugged it off and felt confident she'd figure it out as time passed on.

On the first day of kindergarten, Mrs. Harshberger invited all the adults to stay for the first hour or two of class while the children got acclimated to their new surroundings. Each family also had a little one-on-one time to be introduced to their new teacher. She was an older woman with short blond hair and blue eyes that reminded the Little Girl's Lola that there was something to constantly aspire to in this country. There was no changing the color of their eyes, or hair, or skin, but they can shapeshift without having to change too much of their exterior. Before Mrs. Harshberger left to speak to another family, the Little Girl's Lola and Mom mentioned that she could read English and that she's been taking charge of story time in the house. Mrs. Harshberger gave them a gentle smile and moved on to the next family.

After some mingling, everyone in the classroom settled, and it was time to learn about the classroom rules. Mrs. Harshberger called attention to a large poster board taped to the wall strewn with the class's sacred bylaws. She began to read each rule out loud and followed by asking everyone if they understood. Coming down to the last rule, Mrs. Harshberger remembered what the Little Girl's family told her. She called on the Little Girl and told the class that she knew how to read. "Can you read the last rule?" she asked the Little Girl. "Be kind to others," the Little Girl proudly read.

As the school year commenced, Mrs. Harshberger went about the days teaching the standard curriculum and having one-on-one time here and there throughout the week to go over letter recognition and sight words. The Little Girl had no problem with any of the material, but Mrs. Harshberger thought otherwise. They spent more time on what she sounded like and not the fact that the Little Girl knew her way around letters and words.

The Little Girl was learning so much in this classroom. She soaked up everything her teacher was giving her and was learning how to interact with the other kids. In the coming days, she quickly learned that bringing *arroz caldo* in a thermos incited strange looks from her classmates. She was the only Filipina girl in the classroom, so this was different for the rest of the class. The heavy door to the classroom also seemed to get heavier to open and close. One day, she tried to catch the door before one of her classmates closed it, but she didn't make it. She tried and tried to open it, but couldn't. Asking for help was something she was afraid to do. Her Lola was making her into such a self-sufficient human that asking for someone to open the door felt embarrassing. She wanted to have the strength to open the door on her own but didn't have the muscle to open such a gargantuan door just yet.

A couple of months into the school year, a young woman came into the classroom. Mrs. Harshberger called out a few of the students' names to follow this young woman, as she told the rest of the class they were going to get into story time. The Little Girl's name was called, and she followed the young woman to another classroom on the other side of the school. Among the group were a few of her classmates and other kids from other grades. What was she doing here? The young woman went in and out of speaking English and another language that the Little

Girl did not recognize. They began sounding out letters and words. The Little Girl was very confused, because she already knew every single letter of the alphabet and could successfully put all the letters together to make the words that the young woman was making the class pronounce. The Little Girl was put in an English as a Second Language class. She knew English but didn't look or sound the part of an assimilated American girl.

The Little Girl grew more and more frustrated with each passing ESL class. She wanted to be in story time. Even if she was happy to see this young woman give the same kind of care her Lola gave her when learning to read to the other kids, she knew all of this already. She was fortunate enough to have spent so much time with her Lola and felt confident in what she took from her Lola. She didn't understand why she had to take this supplemental class.

One day, as the young woman rounded up the ESL kids, the Little Girl was fed up. This class was valuable, but it wasn't the class she needed to be in. So, as the class was settling into story time and the small group of kids was leaving for ESL, the Little Girl quietly and sneakily made her way to the back of the classroom behind the bookshelf and hid underneath a table. She belonged in story time. The Little Girl waited with great anxiety to see if she could get away with this act of defiance and wished her fellow ESL classmates could join her under the table. The shuffling of feet going out the door faded into silence, and the classroom found its calm as story time was about to begin. Maybe they mistook her for absent? Who knows? The Little Girl was just relieved she pulled this off. She grabbed her knees into her chest, took a deep breath, and listened to Mrs. Harshberger read, *The Very Hungry Caterpillar*. Quietly. For herself.

In this moment, she began to understand how the life ahead of her would leave her feeling like she wouldn't belong for what she looked like, how she'd sound, what she ate. The doors in this country would always, for her, be heavy. For most of her life, she'd find herself dulling the stories embedded in her skin to appease this country's comfort. Her Lola had to do the same. Eventually, they would let the world slip away and sing in their mother tongue, remembering the joy of what they shared in those months before she tried to open the first of those heavy doors.

Left photo Lola and young Krystle; Right top photo: Krystle as a young girl learning how to read; Right bottom photo: Krystle as an adult with her Lola

Trip To Manila: A Poetry Collection

JACOB MAGALLANES

LAX to MNL

As I fly into the night
The clouds cover the city lights
Through them, you tell me, "Don't worry, baby!"
"I'll still be here, so rest easy."

Your light kindles safety in arms, dainty, yet strong.
I leave you for now, wishing you'd come along.
But instead of heart-aching, I smile.
Thoughts of hugs after being gone a while.

Lolo's Home

As I step through the threshold of my late *lolo's* home
It creaks and groans under the weight of being alone
The time of life and love in this house has gone

Couches and shelves are covered in bed sheets
Caskets for memories which shall never repeat
This was once my ancestors' home, it was never for me

"You'll be back before you know it," I reassure myself
But homesickness racks my mind
I wish so dearly to leave this haunted house behind.

The Cemetery

Hidden on a side street, covered in weeds
Generations of my family lie here in peace.
From loved ones who we still mourn
To centuries-old names I've never heard before.

Yellow-striped butterflies flutter about
Alley-cats and horned beetles roam around.
The life is so vibrant in this memorial to death
Chasing the sadness of this place away with their sounds.

No longer does here, nor *lolo's* home, feel empty.
For all of the experiences of my ancestry
Life and love remains within our minds' memories.

8

Losing Lola

G. CHRIS VILLANASCO

When we arrived in L.A., Mom was contacting people all day as she was hearing about arrangements from Tito Boy. The next day, we tried to absorb the shock of the news and our traveling. We ate at a Filipino restaurant and shared funny stories about Lola. I think we were still dancing around the topic, not wanting to fall apart in a public restaurant. Our *halo halos* made Mom recall selling *halo halo* at their stand back home. She used to like to get the ice because it meant that she could ride the *calesa* back.

When more family arrived, we were joking over dinner with happy memories and our current lives. Mom was filling us in on how Lola was a single mother for a while when Lolo had a job as a high school principal in another town. She ran a little store outside of the school, where they sold lined paper by the sheet and candy by the piece. Lola would go to the wholesaler early in the morning and bring it back to sell during the day. She thought that Lola was a woman always ahead of her time.

More families arrived from DC and Houston. We were still thrilled to see one another. At lunch, we went around and tried to share a good memory or a favorite food from Lola. The weight of the despair was just behind all our smiles. Josh mostly remembered visits where Lola always had something prepared. Angelo remembered a sweet and sour fish, Jasmine called her "the Merienda Queen," and Helen recalled her *estufado*. It was funny. I remember my aunt from England, my dad's sister, saying once that Lola had this tiny kitchen (in the Philippines) but things always came out in big steaming pots.

I recall that when I came to visit once, she told me to sleep in her bed. Well, I of course refused at first, horrified at the idea of letting my grandmother sleep on the couch while I took her bed.

But she said, "No, no please. I have to get up early at 5 a.m. to feed the homeless."

I was of course humbled, and we listened to her wishes as usual. The next morning, I got up late because I was still groggy from my slight jet lag. Lola was gone, and breakfast was on the table. I was so embarrassed that a woman sixty years older than me had more energy than I could muster. She came back from church happy from doing her part. She told me she told each person in line for food to take time after the meal to go to the church and give thanks to the Lord. She quoted, " 'Yes, Ma'am,' they said."

When my cousin San Fran joined us, he shared that he remembered going to school in L.A. and taking the bus to see her. She would always feed him and then fill his bag with food for the next week. They also talked about how Lola liked the liquid drink, Ensure. They all seemed to have the same threads of Lola's generosity and her exuberance. We all had stories.

Some spent the afternoon in Hollywood showing out-of-towners around, shopping, and getting haircuts. Tito Boy and family were making the final arrangements for tomorrow's wake and Monday's funeral. Mom continued to contact people and hear calls of sympathy from relatives in Ohio and Washington, DC.

I got to spend a quiet hour to myself. I felt like the big wave was coming as we could no longer hide what brought us together this time.

Tito Boy arranged for a mass that afternoon at Lola's Catholic church, Immaculate Heart of Mary. He called us to talk about the arrangement of the readers for a mass. He said that I do the first reading and San Fran would do the responsorial psalm, etc., giving everyone a role. He said to talk to the priest at the church.

San Fran and I were the only ones on the program to arrive early, so we went into the church and told the priest and the lecters that we were performing the first reading and the responsorial. It took some time for one of the ladies to find the proper readings for that day's mass, and San Fran and I were getting very nervous to be reading in front of the whole family and a full Saturday mass. We, after all, have both stopped practicing Catholicism. But it would be important for Lola and for her friends to have a mass dedicated to her. So we plodded on.

We made a few mistakes, like moving towards the lectern early, which the priest corrected us on. San Fran was a bit embarrassed by our missteps, but we read our parts pretty smoothly, considering we had ten minutes to prepare.

During the mass, I felt the overwhelming sense of Lola's presence. The attendees of the mass are mostly Filipino, and many are seniors like Lola. Their voices in prayer sounded like they included Lola. I usually have a quandary about taking communion because I have not been to church in years, but I felt a calling to take communion—like it was sharing a feast with Lola. I remembered a time when I was in college, and I came out to spend my winter term with Lola and Lolo. I was helping Lola restock the church with communion supplies and flowers. As she was filling the cabinet with altar wine bottles, she saw that one was almost empty. She said we should finish the bottle. She found some glasses, and we shared a drink of wine together in the back of the church!

As I took a sip of the communal wine this time, I was flooded with Lola's memory as well as Lola's presence. We would not share another glass on Earth. I felt like it was a toast goodbye. I had a sense that my relationship with her was over. Yet, I know she would always be around for every celebration, every sorrow, every moment alone, every gathering for the rest of my life. It was devastating to feel in touch with her faith, her humor, her modernity, and her tradition, and most of all her affection for me and for all of us in that moment.

When we all gathered in the parking lot, Helen and I hugged and cried. She said she felt Lola's presence too, especially as the setting sun came through the stained glass windows and filled the church with light.

ONE FUNNY STORY ABOUT this mass is that neither San Fran nor I were actually scheduled to read! Tito Boy's lineup for readings was for Monday's service at the memorial park, not today's service at Immaculate Heart. Without warning, San Fran and I just took over the church and told the lectors that we were reading! We were so bold and direct that they did not question us. It was like we were bearing Lola's authority. I even carried the book of the Word of the Lord over my head in the procession as the mass began! I was walking in front of the priest.

Tito Boy, Tita Angela, and Tita Ceding almost fell off the couch laughing when we told them how we walked in. We made a mistake—but it was a good mistake. We were supposed to read on Monday, not Saturday. We just took over the mass. Between our laughs, San Fran and I discussed that Lola probably set it up that we would be the ones to participate in the church mass. She was calling us to give thanks to the Lord her way, to acknowledge the church, maybe to call us back, or maybe because she thought it would be funny.

Thankfully, the lectors were friends of Lola, and they just took it in stride. In fact, they coached us. Plus, it made the focus of the mass more on Lola because her family participated. Now, even more grandchildren can participate in the ceremonies commemorating Lola because others could take our regularly scheduled places on Monday. Angelo would do the first reading, and Daniel would do the responsorial psalm.

The heaviest burden would come Sunday morning at the wake. We would see Lola for the first time. I think the anxiety level for everyone was high, and tempers flared, but everyone apologized and forgave each other as we made the final plans. The family would have a private viewing from 9 a.m. to 11 a.m., and the room would be available for all guests from 11 a.m. to 9 p.m.

We all quickly prepared the next day. The chapel was not open yet, but we could see the casket through the frosted glass windows. When they signaled us to come in, I waited for mom and dad as they were greeting the first guests. We entered to see Angelo kneeling and crying, and Mom and I got to have our first vision of Lola in her final state.

It was emotionally devastating. We had to face that her spirit was gone from this body, yet her appearance was still before us.

Mom fell to her knees and started crying, saying, "Thank you, Thank you, Mang, for everything."

We were holding each other's hands very tightly, and I could feel my dad, Angelo, and Jasmine holding us from behind. They each had their own moments with Lola as mom and I retreated to the seats in tears.

I was crying uncontrollably too. I had to face her death and departure. All those feelings I was harboring came flooding out. Yet, I was also saying thank you, and I felt an awesome joy that set us free. She was released from this body that could no longer hold her amazing spirit. She did all she needed to do in this world. She completed her mission on Earth. There was no more for her to do. She leaves triumphant and accomplished in God's eyes. She was liberated from this Earth to see God to enter Heaven. How happy she must be to finally rest and to be with the Lord that she prayed to every day of her life.

When we could finally see through our tears we saw that she looked beautiful and relaxed though small and pallid. Lying on her back, her skin looked smooth. Mom was worried that the funeral home would put on too much make-up, but we only noticed a pale shade of pink on her lips. It was good to feel like she looked as she did in life. Only, I remember watching her sleep in life. She would still be actively dreaming and thinking, turning to find a comfortable position, arranging layers of clothing or sheets. Now, her face looked smooth and her lips were painted light pink. There was no tension, no worry in her face or her body. Her hands were folded, and they were wrapped in a rosary and holding a cross. She had been released from her obligations in this life, and she was prepared to leave, to go to her final rest.

I'm grateful that I went so that I could share the weight of this loss with my family. I feel as if we absorbed the biggest wave of emotions over losing Lola together. I still have smaller bursts of missing her and reminiscing about her, but we all went through the transformation of our relationship with Lola as a family. It made me feel honored to be in this family and to have Lola bring us together again.

9

Death By A Broken Heart

GABBIE AQUINO-ADRIATICO

This pandemic contains so much loss-loss of routine. Loss of jobs. Loss of safety. Loss of schools. Loss of planning. And the one I want to talk about today is the loss of loved ones. New York was hit hard by COVID-19. Hospitals are overwhelmed, frontliners overworked, and it seemed that the entire community lacked PPEs. Two elderly members of my extended family that we called Lolo and Lola lived together in an apartment in New York. From the Philippines to New York, they were always together. They were inseparable. They were each other's best friend.

One morning during the pandemic, Lola wasn't feeling well. She started to throw up. Lolo took her to the hospital and to his disappointment, he was told that only patients were allowed. He was sad that he couldn't go into the hospital with her. Eventually he kissed her and said, "See you later." He went back home.

Lola was diagnosed with COVID-19 on March 31st. And a few hours later, she passed away. The doctor called Lolo with the heartbreaking news. He was devastated. Next thing you know, he was informed that his *mahal*, the love of his life, had to be cremated immediately due to New York having no space with so many people dying from COVID-19. He never got to see her after he took her to the hospital. He never got to say goodbye. He never got to hug her again. And, he did not get the choice of how to bury her.

He was heartbroken.

Lolo got tested for COVID-19 since he was showing symptoms. He was sent home to recover since his symptoms were not as severe. Eventually after a few days, he collapsed in his apartment. He was rushed to the hospital. Several hours later, he died. He was cremated as well. Did Lolo die from COVID-19? Yes. But I think he died more from losing his *mahal,* the love of his life – a phenomena called the broken heart syndrome.

Losing a loved one, especially the death of a spouse, is one of the most painful and stressful experiences a person can experience. It not only impacts the mental health of the individual, but it takes a toll on their physical health as well. And on top of that, during this pandemic, it's difficult to grieve in the ways you are used to since there are many restrictions like not being able to see your family or go to church. The comfort of the grieving practices we once had–hugging one another, holding each other's hands, being in each other's presence, wiping away the tears of loved ones, all had been taken away.

The feelings of loss have made itself a frequent guest during my quarantine experience. Week after week, I hear stories, receive texts from our family group chat, and see the media highlight how much people are losing their lives to COVID-19. At first, I was numb to all of it and would not give myself permission to grieve. I pushed myself to stay "optimistic" about our situation despite learning that over 250,000 people around the world have died from COVID-19. But now it's sinking in. I'm choosing to let it in. I'm choosing to lean into my grief. Because I can't move forward unless I lean into it, right? This week I'm finally letting go of denial and opening my heart to my frequent guests—feelings of loss. I'm learning new ways to cope since I can't be with my family during this time. I'm learning new ways to love my family since we are all states and oceans apart. I'm learning to love through Zoom, Facebook, and group chats.

The past month has been emotionally exhausting. COVID-19 has taken away so much from our lives—our routine, our jobs, our safety, our schools, our plans, and our loved ones. But one thing I have learned from this pandemic is that COVID-19 can't take away our love.

Lolo and Lola from New York refused to be apart from one another. They're known to be the "forever loves" in our extended family.

Our family group chat on Facebook messenger has daily notifications from my *titas*, aunts, *titos*, uncles, *pinsans*, cousins, and even my *lolos*, grandpas, and *lolas*, grandmas, sending notes of encouragement and forwarding images that convey how much they miss the family. They send daily prayer chains and share links to Catholic masses online. Our love for one another during this pandemic has grown more and more. *Yun pagmamahal namin sa isat isa, hindi nawawala.* The love that we have for each other will never go away.

Later on, when it's safe to travel, my family will bring Lolo and Lola's ashes back to the Philippines, and so they can be together again with their loved ones there.

COVID-19 may have changed the way we grieve, but it did not change the love between Lolo and Lola. COVID-19 cannot take away the love of my family.

10

My Ancestor, From The Great Beyond

ROYAL SUMIKAT

It all started with this message in a group chat on **Wednesday, March 11, 2020.** Ate Christy asked us, "Bataan Memorial death March canceled. If anyone wants to do a walk with me this weekend, I will do it anyways here in Houston." The Bataan Memorial Death March is an annual 14 mile march that happens at White Sands Missile Range in New Mexico. It honors the heroic service members who defended the Philippine Islands during World War II, sacrificing their freedom, health, and in many cases, their lives. Over 75,000 Filipino and American troops in Bataan were forced to make a perilous 70-mile march to prison camps. The marchers made the trek through intense heat and were subjected to harsh treatment by Japanese guards. Thousands perished.

Ate Christy has attended this march annually for the past 6 years in New Mexico. Unfortunately, large gatherings and events were being canceled left and right as precautionary measures against COVID-19. Despite the cancellation, she made it happen here in Houston with us. I texted her back that, "I'm down to walk 14 miles with you."

It's March 14th, Saturday. 6:00 a.m.

Joining with us was Ate Christy, Cybil, Jenah, Trish, and Christian on my very first long distance march! Ate Christy asked if we wanted to dedicate the march to family members who served or are currently serving. None of the family members I know have ever served in the military, but the Philippines WAS invaded by Japan during WWII — so I'm sure someone in my family line did.

Lots of positive omens appeared during our trek. The march felt like a lifetime in that we shared many stories between us, saw numerous interesting sights, and learned a lot from each other. One thing I learned about during the walk was the Filipino Veterans Of World War II Congressional Gold Medal Act. From Congresswoman, Tulsi Gabbard's press release:

"The United States is forever grateful for the service, bravery, and perseverance of the more than 200,000 Filipino and Filipino American soldiers that served our country during World War II. These loyal and courageous soldiers suffered hardships, fought bravely, and sacrificed greatly, with many giving up their lives alongside their American counterparts throughout the war, yet their service was left unrecognized in the United States for decades. Today, these brave soldiers are finally receiving the recognition they earned and deserve, and join the ranks of heroic units like the Tuskegee Airmen and Hawaii's own 442nd/100th Infantry Battalion as we honor

MY ANCESTOR, FROM THE GREAT BEYOND   47

them with the Congressional Gold Medal—our nation's highest civilian honor."

It turns out, if you are a World War II veteran or a living relative of one who has passed, you can apply for this Congressional Gold Medal with proof of service. And when the application is approved, they hold a medal ceremony to honor them at the annual Bataan Memorial Death March.

THE FOLLOWING **MONDAY, MARCH 16, 2020** after our march, I saw an owl relative early in the morning while letting the dogs out. I've never seen an owl outside of captivity, especially in Houston. Owls symbolize good and bad omens, depending on the culture. Some believe they're harbingers of death, wisdom, protection, or major changes in the coming days. I'd say the owl omen foretold my coming days.

That afternoon, a company-wide email was sent out announcing office closures until March 30th (LOL). We were told to bring everything from the office that would enable us to work remotely. After consuming hella news about the quarantine and worrying myself – that evening, I was browsing Instagram and saw a magical practitioner I follow, solaristhehiipriestess, burning money in a pot. She had post about burning ancestor money.

I had so many questions! What is ancestor money? Why is she burning it? And why do you have to buy...money? I did what any curious person would do who didn't want to ask potentially dumb questions—I looked at the post's comment section. And boom, here's a breadcrumb on @alinaax's instagram "The other day I was at a store where they sell a bunch of Joss stuff..." Joss stuff...hm, okay, okay, cool, cool. Interesting. I Googled "joss" and the auto predict drop down appeared: *joss–paper, joss–money*. I clicked on the first link that popped up and here's the basic summary from Nations Online.

The spirit money is a modernization of joss paper, an afterlife monetary paper offering used in traditional Chinese ancestor veneration. In order to ensure that ancestors or ghosts have proper items in the afterlife, their relatives send them paper and papier-mâché presents. The burning of the spirit money and paper objects allows for the object to be transferred to the ancestors and ghosts, materializing in the afterlife and even increase in value.[1] I fell into a research rabbit hole and found online magic shops that sell numerous denominations of joss money—American dollars, Yen, and even getting creative with currency using deities from different spiritual pantheons.

By this time I was on Etsy, wondering if joss paper existed for Philippine Pesos. I searched for *Philippine Pesos joss money*. Nope.

Okay, how about *Philippine Pesos joss paper*? Nothing relevant.

Alright, let's try *Philippine Pesos ancestral money*. Zero.

At this point, I just wanted to make the search as broad as possible so I typed *Philippine Money*.

And then a search result titled "Philippines Death Sentence Gu..." with an image of Philippines money caught my eye. Excuse me? Death sentence??? My interest was thoroughly piqued. From the description of the result, it basically described how during World War II, the Japanese declared that any Philippines money existing at the time was no longer valid, and the Japanese

---

1. https://www.missmelindasmetaphysicalservices.com/blog/joss-paper-history-and-modern-use

created their own currency to use in the Philippines. In the meantime, Filipino guerrilla fighters decided to print illegal emergency notes since there was a shortage in physical money, creating the forbidden guerrilla money. That gave me goosebumps. Of course I had to get it! How synchronous is it that I just did this memorial march to honor the warriors of WWII, and this came up in my reality? So many people risked their lives to defy the Japanese by circulating this currency. It could just be me, but the hairs stood on the back of my neck as I held these notes.

On **Friday, March 20, 2020**, I called my parents to check in with them and see how they were adjusting to the pandemic shutdown. Before getting off the phone, I asked my mom if she knew any family members who served in the military past or present. She said no, but she did say that my dad's grandfather was in the military. She hands the phone to my dad. I asked my dad the same question. He said, "Yeah, he was an American citizen, you know. He served in the U.S. Army during World War II." So casual. This was big news for me.

"What? How come you never told me this?" I said.

"You never asked," said my dad.

Upon talking about this with other Filipinx folks, I realize I'm not the only one who has elders who need to be asked to share stories of the past or pry it out of them. I hope we can shift this. Our stories are incredibly important.

So I asked, "Where was he stationed? What did he do? Do you have any pictures?"

My dad, a man of few words, said, "I don't know that much. He was a POW and was stationed in Bataan."

"Oh, you mean the same Bataan where the death march happened?" I said out loud.

I asked if his family had any records of his service: pictures, certificates, and paperwork. Again, mostly 'I don't knows,' but he did say he saw one of his sister's post a photo of his father on her Facebook a while back. Okay, this is something!

The next day, I called my dad and asked for my Great Lolo's (grandfather) name. He gave it to me. So I started my Google search. Our last names are pretty unique but as hard as I was looking, nothing was showing up for me. I was starting to get worried because every time I searched for World War II archives, the 1973 fire kept popping up in the search list.

Apparently, there was a fire that occurred at the National Archives office in St. Louis, Missouri in July of 1973. It happened in a section of the building that housed Army and Air Force records between 1912 to 1964. About 80% of the records were lost without any duplicates ever made. Which means, there's a possibility that my great grandpa's information perished with the fire.

Then, an hour later my dad calls back.

"Hey, I gave you the wrong name. I forget my father is a Jr. and he went by the same name as my father."

"Thanks. I'll search with that name," I said.

Then, my dad said, "I already found him."

"What? Where?" I said in shock.

My dad gave me the link to a Pacific POW Roster and immediately I hit CTRL+F and typed our last name. And there he was, among thousands of names that might not

MY ANCESTOR, FROM THE GREAT BEYOND 51

have been uttered in decades—in a sea of C's, my great grandfather, Corporal Regino Cabio. I stared at his name for minutes, just bawling my eyes out. There he is.

But I needed to know more. Now equipped with his actual name, I was able to find him in the National Archives and thankfully, his information wasn't affected by the fire. It says the date report year was 1942 and the latest report year was 1945. Does that mean he was a POW for 3 years?

I clicked on the other links that showed up in my search and came across Fold3.com, a site that provides scans and images of military records. I signed up for the 10 day free trial (and completely forgot to cancel so I was charged $75) and searched for my Great Lolo's name. I found these images filed under *Organization Index to Pension Files of Veterans Who Served Between 1861 and 1900, 1949 – 1949.*

I have so many questions.

My dad said he was born in 1901. In the first pension card, it says he enlisted in 1918, when he was 17 and was discharged in 1919. At the corner of the card, it is stamped with the words *World War*.

The second card says he enlisted in 1919 and was discharged in 1925. But the invalid sections for both cards were populated, meaning he survived this particular war but became sick, incapacitated, or disabled.

The date of filing for these cards were 1927.

Ate Christy did show me a wikipedia on Philippines Legislature passing the Declaration of Purposes in 1919, a transitional time for the Philippines to determine their freedom and sovereignty. This might have explained the different dates of his service. This could mean he must've fought in the First World War, got sick, and then he was drafted in the Second War at the age of forty-one! He must have been a real badass.

My dad said my grandfather was already born when my Great Lolo was drafted. It makes me wonder, what my great grandmother did while he was away fighting and the Japanese were invading the Philippines? Did she have to survive in hiding with her children? Did she do it all by herself or with others? Did the United States protect the families of soldiers?

After all the searching and falling into numerous rabbit holes, this left me with one more task. Now that I found him in a couple of official lists, I got on FilVetRep.org to see what qualifies as acceptable documents to register him for a Congressional Medal of Honor.

ON FRIDAY, MARCH 20, 2020, I downloaded the form, filled it out, and sent it to Ate Christy since she is the Region Director for the registry. Here is the email exchange between me and my dad, Merlito, with Ate Christy, and Nonie:

Ate Christy,

Good evening. Please see attached documents and proof of my great grandfather, Regino Cabio's service during World War II. His birthday was in October 1901. My father said it was PROBABLY the 24th. But he is sure of the month and year. Pictures of his enlistment records were found on https://www.fold3.com/. I was also able to find his information on this link below and by searching for "Cabio" here. Please let me know if you need anything else.

Royal

MY ANCESTOR, FROM THE GREAT BEYOND

Hi Nonie-

I would like to put forth the below applicant for approval. I think there is ample evidence. Do you concur?

Regards, Christy

Hi Christy/Merlito,

Yes, ample of evidence to warrant approval. Merlito and Royal, we can include your grandpa to our next Congressional Gold Medal Award Ceremony, Las Cruces Convention Center, Las Cruces, NM, in conjunction with the Bataan Death march, White Sands Missile Range in March 2021.

Best, Nonie

I was crying when I was reading the email over and over. I was shaken. Not even two weeks ago, I marched without any knowledge of family who served and only honored ancestors through intention. And here he is now, confirming his existence and in the process, will be honored with a Congressional Medal of Honor. It was as if my participation in the Memorial March sent a spiritual ping to his spirit beeper (look, I don't know the ancestral realm and I currently can't come up with a better analogy) into the Great Beyond and it strengthened our connection to each other.

Not only that, he couldn't have reached out at a more relevant time. With economic uncertainty, the pandemic, and this unprecedented reality—it's as if he was reminding me that the blood that flows through me is from an ancient line of survivors and warriors. And if he survived as a POW in World War II, I can get through this too.

Maraming salamat for the breadcrumbs, Lolo. Thank you for your protection. Thank you for your messages. Thank you.

May I be the living altar for you and the ancestral line who supports me.

MY ANCESTOR, FROM THE GREAT BEYOND

Top photo: bottom row- Royal, Jenah, Trisha, Ate Christy; top row- Christian, Cybil; Middle left photo: Royal's honor sign, photo credit to Christian Toledo; Middle right photo: The Congressional Gold Medal awarded posthumously to Ate Christy's ancestor, Francisco "Ecoy" Panis, photo credit to Christian Toledo; Bottom left photo: Marching together in the city of Houston, photo credit to Christian Toledo; Bottom right photo: Owl as an omen

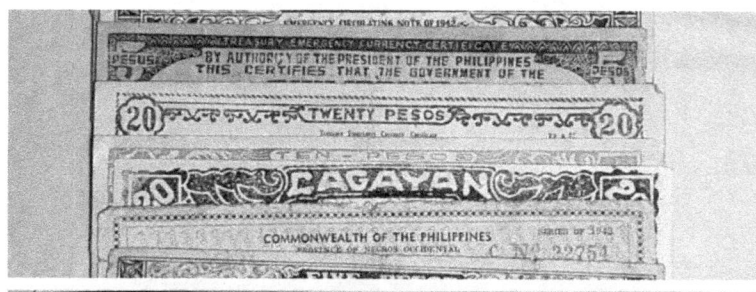
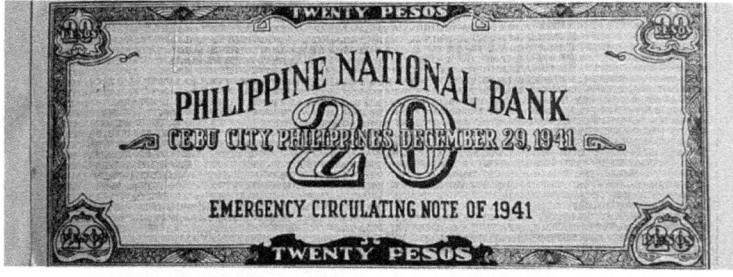
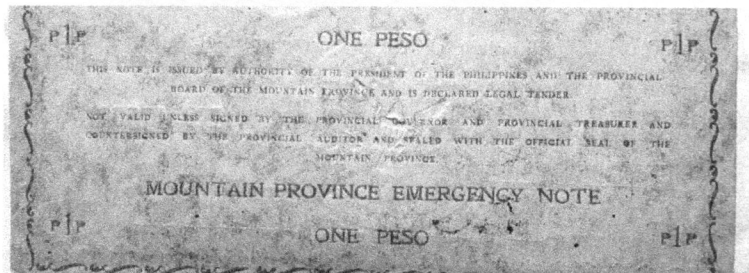
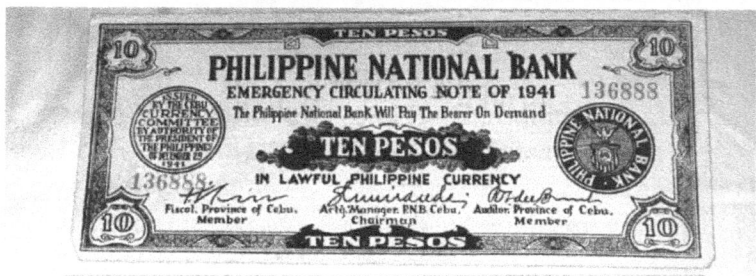

The Philippines Emergency Notes, known as Guerrilla Money, Royal purchased online

MY ANCESTOR, FROM THE GREAT BEYOND

Great Lolo Regino Cabio's military information from the Organization Index to Pension Files of Veterans Who Served Between 1861 and 1900, 1949-1949 found on www.Fold3.com

11

Dear Inay

CYBIL JOY PALLUGNA-SAENZ

I've been working on this letter
in my mind for decades,
But I only started writing
it down moments ago.

So many times
I've bit my tongue
to avoid "the hard" talks.

The ones that would
change the dynamic
of our relationship
forever.

The ones that would
release all of
our pent up emotions:
Rage
Regret
Remorse

Jealousy
Disappointment

The ones that would
reveal to you my:
Admiration
Appreciation
Fulfillment
Consideration
Respect

The words I wanted to say
would disappear before
I had a chance to say them,
until now...

Because I see YOU.

You came to this country
with Daddy and Ate
to escape the oppression
of Filipino Martial Law.

You started a new life
in a foreign country,
thousands of miles away
from all that you've known.

That must've been so scary
But not as scary
as living under
the thumb
of a tyrannical government
and unjust dictator
or
the uncertainty of
a future in a corrupt country.

You took that leap of faith
at the tender age of 28
with a baby in tow

to find a better life
in the land of the free

But little did you know
that the arduous journey
was really meant for
you to meet me.

I was born a year after
you arrived in this distant place
conceived after a night of
galavanting around
Chicago's sparkling lights.

but that wasn't your intention.

I was a fussy baby.
Always sick.
Always crying.
Always needing attention.

My nickname is Cee Bee,
which I thought was
just a shorter version
of my name.

But I found out years later
that it stood for "Cry Baby".

I was allergic to almost everything
and was close to dying
when you fed me peanuts
before my second birthday.

You would tell me repeatedly:

"You were an accident."
"We found you in a garbage can."
"It was only supposed to be your sister."

All at the tender age of six.
This narrative stuck with me
throughout my life
And made me feel more
like a burden instead
of a lovechild.

I would always feel like
I wasn't good enough
and would punish myself by

Cutting
Being in abusive relationships
Attempting suicide

Now, 30 years later
from that night you
discovered me
after a twelve hour shift
at the hospital

Bleeding from my wrist,
lying on my bed
unconscious from
an overdose
of unknown pills
I grabbed from
the medicine cabinet,

I finally see YOU.

I see YOU in myself
when I am with my own children,
my own family.

I see YOU come out of me
when I am frustrated,
angry,
upset,
enraged.

I see YOU
when I respond to you
in the same way you
respond to me.

And that's when YOU
see yourself reflected back at YOU.

We are one person, Inay,
and we both want to change

But the only way for us to do that
is to break the mirror of
systemic generational trauma.

I see YOU
and I want YOU
to release US
from these chains!

Beat out the reflection of
yourself that you see in me.

I allow you to do that.

I need you to do that.

I want you to shatter this
cycle of pain!

I am sorry it's taken a pandemic
and a brush with COVID-19
to have the courage
to dig up this long overdue conversation.

I am sorry it's taken me
so long to figure out
what I've wanted to say to you,
what I've needed from you.

I am sorry it's taken me
so long to finally see YOU.

To see YOU
as a woman,
a person,
a human,
and not just
my MOTHER.

12

Mommy's Kuwento

NOURELIZA MONTIFAR

Here it goes. This is the kuwento of my first love, my mom. I remember the day when I was 5 years old and was able to write: "I love you Mommy." It was one of my proudest moments and I wrote Mommy many love letters with just that one sentence. Each time Mommy received a letter she would always have that same gaze in her eyes full of love and happiness.

Mommy was the eldest of seven children. She grew up in the Philippines. Her father passed away when she was 12 years old. His passing made her feel that she needed to step up to the plate to help take care of her six younger siblings. Throughout Mom's life you could see and feel that she had that heavy weight of responsibility on her shoulders. Her family was poor. My grandmother did her very best to take care of her kids, but sometimes it was not enough financially. When Mommy was a child, she told me that she would go work at various relative's homes to help clean or iron clothes so that she would get paid to help her family. While she was in school, she couldn't afford her textbooks, so she used to borrow them from her friends that were a grade before her. Mommy was a very determined little girl. She did whatever it took so that she could finish school. She did not let her financial status determine her fate. With her efforts she received a scholarship in college, which helped tremendously with her tuition. She graduated with her bachelors degree.

Even till the days when Mom was an adult, she was still a very determined woman who always kept her family's best interest in mind. She worked in the U.S. and she would send funds or boxes to help her family in the Philippines. Mommy is one of the most selfless, caring, loving, and generous people I know. I remember as a kid whenever we would walk home on the avenue and she would see a homeless person, she wouldn't even think twice or hesitate to help. She treated the homeless with the respect that any person deserves. She would offer to buy them lunch. Seeing that as a kid had a strong impact on me. Imagine, my mom was showing love to a total stranger. It just gave my heart that warm fuzzy feeling inside. It taught me how to share my blessings and how to show love to others.

Mommy was always a giver. I remember how she would take the time to make *pancit* and *lumpia* then she would bring it to work and sometimes bring it to my teachers at school. She was proud to be a Filipino and she showed that through her food. All her coworkers and my teachers loved her. Mom's giving spirit always created this warm and positive environment for me and my siblings while we were growing up. She showed us what it meant and looked like to be kind and spread love to the *kapwa*, to the people.

I really looked up to my mom. She is such a beautiful person and has a beautiful gentle soul. She was my role model and was someone that I aspired to become. My mom always spoke about being positive and always smiling. She was very stoic. I know deep down inside she carried some aches and pains, but those were things she didn't want to burden us with. Later on in life, I found out that she suffered through some depression. Mental health was a taboo topic so she never really outright said aloud. It was later as an adult that I realized it.

Mom had some very tough times in her life and those experiences got her to where she is today. She worked hard to provide for her family back home in the Philippines and she provided for us. Mom immigrated to the U.S. back in the 1980s. She wanted to be a school teacher, but her uncle convinced her to work in the medical field because he said that the medical field employees were always in demand and they got paid better. It always broke my heart when she told me that story because she sacrificed her dream and passion of being a school teacher so that she could work in the medical field to help provide a better life for her family back home. Again, there goes Mommy being selfless.

Around 2006, Mommy was diagnosed with breast cancer. She worked the graveyard shift in the hospital for 25 years, and they say that may have correlated to her stress which caused the cancer. I remember that day when we received the news that Mommy was diagnosed with breast cancer. As kids, my siblings and I thought the worst case scenario and thought there was a great chance we could lose our mom. With Mom being the positive and stoic person that she is, she reminded us that we should pray and be positive. She reassured us that everything would be fine, and that it was. Mom had a mastectomy of her one breast. I remember she came home with a JP drain and I would help her empty it and clean around her surgical site. Once her wounds healed, she was left with only one breast and a scar. She never directly said it but I could feel that she lost some of her confidence, and she didn't feel one hundred percent beautiful as she did before. Again that didn't deter her. She continued on with her positive attitude, and thank God she has been cancer free ever since.

MOMMY'S KUWENTO

As a kid I remember Mommy used to have a counter of at least ten different medications. She had one for high blood pressure, one for high cholesterol, she had one for being a pre-diabetic, she had vitamins, and the list went on. Then there was one day when she was just sick and tired of taking all the medications. Looking back now as an adult, I now realize that Mom was going through a time of depression where she just wanted to give up and not take her meds. It was just too much for her. Then her doctor even told her that there may be a chance that she would have to take insulin in the future if she didn't make lifestyle changes during that time. It really worried Mommy and I guess she was scared of the unknown. It seemed as though she was in disbelief that diabetes could happen to her. I remember as a kid, we were in her room and she was just expressing to me her worries and the thought of her possibly having to inject herself with insulin in the future. It stressed her out.

Fast forward, by the time Mommy got out of her depression and decided to do something about it, it was a bit too late. One day Mom's blood sugars got so high that the blood sugar machine couldn't read it and they had to do blood work in order to get a reading. It was well over five hundred. I lived in another state by then and I still remember that day when my sister called me in a panic. She said that she was really worried about Mommy because she peed herself in bed and she was acting delusional. She said that Mommy was not herself, and when she was in the bathroom, she was using the bar of soap as a computer mouse acting like she was at work. She didn't seem to know where she was. And then she soiled herself. That's when we decided to take her to the hospital. During Mom's stay they were able to stabilize her blood sugar, thank God.

Mom was able to recover and she ended up filing for early retirement. It was a blessing in disguise how everything played out. A few years after Mom's retirement we noticed her memory was a little off. She would repeat herself several times and she would forget events that happened recently during the day. We didn't think anything of it. So we carried on with life. Then it seemed like Mom was continuously being forgetful to the point where she couldn't remember if she took her medicine. It reminded us of when my grandmother, who was diagnosed with Alzheimer's in her mid sixties, acted the same way.

Fast forward, we moved Mommy to stay and live with me. From there I took care of her and was able to get a diagnosis from a neurologist. Mom had mild cognitive impairment. It was a step down from dementia. It broke my heart, but I was happy to accept reality and the truth for what it was. Mom was around sixty three and I was 27, my sister 25, and my brother 23. We were still young adults. None of us were married or had kids yet. It hurt because it felt almost like we lost our mom. When I was younger, I always looked forward to Mommy being retired and actually being able to spend quality time with her telling stories. She always used to say, "When I retire, I will cook all your favorite foods and we will spend lots of time together." It hurts because now it feels like I don't have my mom who I can run to for advice about life. Mommy is not there for me to run into her arms and cry and tell me that everything is going to be ok. I no longer have a mommy who gives those back rubs that always gave you the feeling of comfort and safety since I was a child. No home cooked meals. No one to help me take care of my kids 24/7. No more surprises. No more heart to heart talks. No more long hours of conversation.

Instead, the roles were switched. Now, I became the mom and I had to mature and grow up a bit faster. I miss my mom everyday. Sometimes I just imagine what it would have been like if that never happened and Mom had her full memory. It just makes me more motivated to take care of my health so that I can be there for my kids long term neurologically. I miss my mom. I love her. It's hard sometimes to think that I have my mom physically there, but sometimes she just feels like a shell of herself—and I'm missing her. It's as if I lost a big piece of her and she is not all there. Yes I am very blessed and happy that she is alive, but this is a reminder to all parents out there, please take care of your health. Diabetes is serious and can have many long term effects. Diabetes is common especially in the Filipino community. Please take care of yourself so that you can be there for the long run. And to all the adult kids out there, give your parents extra love. Give them that extra hug. Visit them. Spend quality time with them. Listen to their stories with unrushed, undivided attention. You never know, in the blink of an eye, they can lose their memory or they will go to heaven. I miss my mom everyday. I live and reminisce with the memories of "mommy" in my childhood. And I accept Mommy for how she is now. I love her and will continue to shower her with all the love and care that she bestowed upon us as kids.

Dear Mommy, you are a wonderful role model to my siblings and me. We will continue to honor your legacy of kindness and unselfish love. Although the roles may have changed, we will continue to shower you with all the love you poured on us. We love you so much. I love you so much. And I miss you.

13

Huwag Buksan Ang Pinto

JERMUEL P. MANARIN

Alas tres ng umaga nang ako'y gising pa
Binabantayan ang pintong may problema sa pagsasara
Sa takot na may dumating na 'di inaasahang mga bisita
At makita ang magulo kong sala.

Ilang sandali ako ay may narinig
Sa labas ng pinto doon nanggagaling ang tinig
Aking sinilip, taong nakatayo't may tindig
Kumakatok at tila may nais ipahiwatig.

"Sandali, teka, diyan ka muna!"
Wika ko sa kumakatok na bisita
"Sandali, teka, 'wag na muna!"
Magulo ang sala at 'di ko pa kayang ipakita.

"Sandali, teka, lumayo ka muna!"
Sarili ko'y takot at hindi pa handa

HUWAG BUKSAN ANG PINTO

"Sandali, teka, umalis ka na!"
Pakiusap ko dahil wala akong tiwala.

Ako'y tumayo at pumunta sa harap ng pinto
Ito'y pinalitan ng mas mahigpit na kandado
Maging mga bintana'y aking sinarado
Upang 'di makapasok ang bisitang nagkukunwaring interesado.

Aking pinto'y 'wag niyo nang buksan
Sala ko'y magulo pa at batid ko'y ayaw niyong tignan
Aayusin ko ito at 'wag niyo na akong pagmasdan
'Wag na mangulit at nawa kayo'y makiramdam.

Don't Open The Door

English Translation

At three in the morning when I was still awake
Watching the door that had trouble closing
Fearing that some unexpected guests had arrived
And seeing my messy living room.

For a moment I heard
Outside the door there comes sound of a voice
I peered, a person standing with a posture
Knocking and seeming to want to convey something.

"Wait a minute, please stay there!"
I said to the knocking guest
"Wait a minute, not yet!"
The living room is messy and I can't show it yet.

"Wait a minute, distance yourself first!"
I myself am scared and not ready
"Wait a minute, go away!"
I'm begging you because I have no confidence.

I stand up and go to the front of the door
It was replaced with a tighter lock
Even the windows I closed
So that the guest pretending to be interested can't come in.

My door, don't you open it
My living room is a mess, I don't want to look at it
I will fix it and don't judge me anymore
I won't repeat it, please understand.

14

Am I An Introvert?

DUSTIN DOMINGO

AM I AN INTROVERT? It's an honest question I've asked myself recently. Through grade school and college, I had always thought of myself as such. It's a descriptor that others have assigned to me. It's how I've often labeled myself. However, in more recent years I've found myself emerging from my shell and I've appreciated the energy I get from positive interactions with others. This is especially true as spaces become more queer or more ethnically diverse. The reality is that the experiences I've had coming of age as a gay Filipino shaped me to become one who strayed away from others and to actively work towards becoming invisible to mainstream society.

Ring

Ring

One evening, when I was a young boy, I was at home and heard the telephone ring. My mother was cooking *arroz caldo* for dinner, and my father was watching the evening news. With my parents' permission, I picked up the brick sized cordless phone in the kitchen and held it to my ear.

"Um. Hello?" I laughed.

A warm voice from a kind woman responded, "Hi. May I speak to your daddy?"

"Okay. He's right here. Just a second." I handed the phone to my father and returned my attention to a coloring book I'd been mastering at the dining table. I loved experimenting with colors. I'd learned to color within the lines, but often thought about coloring outside of them.

After a short moment, my dad hung up the phone and laughed hysterically in my direction. Through tears of laughter he said, "My coworker thought my son...was my *daughter.*"

His punchline hit me hard in the gut. In that moment, I wasn't sure why, but I felt shame. I'd learned not to speak to strangers or to engage with new people.

Ring

Ring

A couple of years later I found myself as a 5th grade visitor to a 3rd grade classroom as part of a mentorship and helping-hand program facilitated by my elementary school. As the first school bell of the day rang through the halls, I stepped into Ms. Maybe's classroom. A line of much smaller children formed outside by the entrance.

I began my visitor assignment by chatting with Ms. Maybe. She was a young white woman with long blond hair. I was already comfortable with her as she was my former teacher from when I was in her 3rd grade class a couple of years prior. As the younger children waited patiently by the door to be welcomed for the day, Ms. Maybe and I caught up quickly and discussed the tasks that needed to be accomplished around the classroom.

AM I AN INTROVERT?

"It's so great to see you again, Dustin!" Her nose crinkled upwards.

Little eyes peered through the door. The children were attentive, absorbing every word and interaction between me and their teacher.

"Good morning and thank you, Ms. Maybe." I was ready to feel useful. "How can I help?" I asked eagerly.

She handed me a stack of blue and beige plastic boxes with lids. She directed me with a smile, "These are empty baby wipe containers." She pointed at the sink and performed a sort of pantomime of scrubbing and peeling, "I need you to please clean these and remove the labels."

Considering her choice of vibrant yellow and orange butcher paper used to decorate the walls, it was obvious that Ms. Maybe was both artistic and resourceful. She was likely to repurpose these containers to hold crayons, markers, colored pencils and the like. Prepping these plastic boxes to become shiny new repositories for art supplies was a significant job that I was willing and able to take. Art was important to me after all.

Ms. Maybe left me to it. As I skipped to the classroom sink to get started, she proceeded to the doorway and sincerely greeted each student individually. One by one, children scuttled into the classroom and explored their surroundings before finding their seats.

Meanwhile, I covered the drain with a black plug and tugged at the faucet lever to allow a thin stream of water to fill the sink. I did my best to submerge the containers under water and pumped a few globs of soap into the sink and onto my hands. I lathered bubbles between my little fingers in hopes that it would aid me in scraping any adhesive gunk off each plastic surface. As I used my fingernails to begin scraping away at the labels, I felt a curious presence around me. I looked over my right shoulder and I locked eyes with two 3rd grade blue eyed boys standing side by side; they stood only a few feet behind me. The warm water continued to fall from the spout and the soapy bubbles slowly rose.

The boys giggled and asked, "Are you a boy or a girl?"

By that time in my life, I recognized those words as a variation of a familiar question. It was the type of question that inherently made me question my identity and made me internalize homophobic attitudes.

Though this was a familiar question, it shocked me. With a furrowed brow and frustrated face, I ignored the rising water level and turned around. "I'm a boy!" I exclaimed.

"Oh. Because you talk like a girl!" The younger children scurried away to report back to their friends watching from across the classroom.

I turned around and got back to work. From that moment, I knew it was best to talk as little as possible. I feared the accusations of talking like a girl or acting like a girl. These sorts of inquiries evolved over time to become more direct and unkind iterations of *are you gay?* Boys were not meant to be effeminate, I learned. Boys were not meant to be gay.

I WENT THROUGH MY formative years with few friends because I simply felt that it was in my best interest to keep to myself and to withhold trust from anyone. Let's call it an act of self-preservation or a coping strategy. After many years of this retreating behavior, I realized that I was feeling drained of energy and joy. And so while I learned to become introverted, perhaps I have always been extroverted. Perhaps because of my socialization, I learned to characterize myself as introverted and in a cyclical fashion, I adopted behaviors that only reinforced that perception.

As I continue to age, I've found solidarity with others who are part of the LGBTQIA+ community. I've shared my experiences with other Filipinos and Asian Americans. I realize that who I am and who I've become is valid and worthy. I've engaged in activities that empower and support those, like me, who are unlearning silence or invisibility. I've become a mentor to those seeking support to navigate the nuances of our reality. Through this, I'm learning more about who I am. I've learned that I do in fact crave human interaction beyond the institutions of education and the workplace. I enjoy being in fellowship with others, especially those with similar lived experiences. So with that in mind, I declare in this moment: *I am not an introvert.*

15

My Own Privilege

TRISHA MORALES

The night before, we were celebrating Jenah's birthday in her family's backyard, perfectly located next to a lake south of Houston, in a suburb called Pearland, Texas. Seated on brand-new patio furniture, the air smelled like fire pit and BBQ. A string of lights hovered above us, as if to protect us that night. We were able to enjoy each other's company without worry, (except mosquito eating us alive–but of course, we were lucky enough to have plant-based repellent spray).

At 8 a.m. my alarm went off—I was tired, wanting to just stay comfortably in my bed, I knew I needed to wake up and get ready. My friends and I planned to go to the *Families Belong Together* march to fight family separation. Several hundreds of people met on Saturday, June 30, 2018 at Houston City Hall to protest–the past few weeks have been especially heart-rending, with news about the White House detaining immigrant families and separating children from their parents. This is not the first time in U.S. history that the state tore apart families for its own gain and to suppress an undesirable population. We must not forget indigenous genocide and the cultural erasure of indigenous peoples through boarding schools, slavery, lynchings, and police brutality, as well as the many years of immigrant detention that preceded this. American amnesia is strong, particularly when the consequences are inconvenient for those who have not been personally impacted.

Here is 2019 data from American Civil Liberties Union (ACLU) to show the family separation crisis in the U.S.:

> *1. The children are sent to 121 different detention or care centers in 17 states throughout the country, often hundreds or thousands of miles away from where their parents are held.*

> *2. Of the initial pool of 2,654 separated children, the majority was male (64.5 percent). 1,033 of them were under the age of ten when they were detained, including 103 under five.*

> *3. The median length of detention so far is 154 days — more than five months.*

I drove towards the city, and decided to park right next to the city hall – $15 parking. My friends and I sat in the car with cardboard posters, and sharpie pens and wrote messages like: "Families belong together," and "We see you, we hear you, we won't abandon you," all iterations of what our society should already be.

When we arrived at city hall, it was a shock to see the number of people gathered downtown. Due to the summer heat, Houstonians normally keep themselves indoors. As we started marching, the wind was silent and motionless, the sun was bright but burning, and I imagined a cold bath repeatedly. Sweat ran down my forehead and back as I wondered how many miles it took for countless refugees to find safety by desert, mountain, river, or ocean. To find a home, a sanctuary away from their far-off motherland—to feel safe with their friends on a twilight night on a patio they worked hard for; because I know that under the same night sky, families are being broken apart.

I reflected on my own journey, the days I felt abandoned, the days I felt like I didn't belong in specific spaces, and how even when I did have a "home" there were still moments that felt foreign. I've thought many times about my own mother's journey, the perils for a young woman leaving her home country to live a better life —mostly I've thought about her sorrow, the pain of having to leave loved ones and friends she would rarely see again.

The dichotomy of the night before and the day after, speaks volumes here in America. We have the privilege to step outside and inside that zone.

I'm here to acknowledge my own privilege—as a Filipnx womxn, middle-class, able-bodied citizen.

16

Bangon

CHEZKA LADDARAN

Alam kong dumating ka na sa oras na
Pakiramdam mo pinag laruan ka ng mundo
Binugbog ka ng tadhana
At para bang hindi ka na nila binigyan ng pagkakataon
Upang bumangon at makabangon.

Alam kong hirap na hirap kang mag simula
Na sa tuwing susubukan mong bumangon
May hihila sayong pababa
At sasabihin nila ang mga katagang "hindi mo naman kaya"

Pakiramdam mo unti-unti kang pinatay ng sakit
Unti-unti kang ginawang manhid
Wala ka nang ibang maramdaman kung hindi bigat at pighati

Nagawa mo ng saktan ang iyong sarili
Mga sugat na ikaw mismo ang may gawa
Mga dugo na ikaw ang nag patulo sa iyong katawan
Sinugatan mo ang iyong katawan, Binahiran ng dugo ang mga kamay

Pero hindi... Hindi nila alam...
Hindi nila alam na mas sugatan ka sa loob
Mas nagdurugo ka sa loob
Wasak na Wasak ka sa loob

Mga gabing walang ibang maririnig kung hindi ang mga hikbi
Nagmamakaawa na sana naman mawala na ang sakit
Pag susumamo sa Kanya na tama na dahil hindi mo na kaya.

Mga araw na wala ng liwanag
Araw na wala ng bukas
Mga araw na wala ng buhay, at
Buhay na wala ng buhay

Tila ba'y nawalan ka na ng pag asa
Tuluyan kang naligaw sa lugar na minsan tinawag mong tahanan
Tuluyan kang na punit na parang bang papel
Tuluyan ka ng inanod at nag patangay sa mga malalaking alon

Hanggang sa isang araw nagising ka sa sikat ng araw
Muli mo syang nakita, muli mong nakita ang sikat ng araw
Mga araw na minsan ay tinaguan ka...
Liwanag na pinag damutan ka...

Sa iyong pagka bagsak at sa iyong muling pag mulat
Nakita mo sila... Nakita mo ang mga kamay na minsan mong tinalikuran
Mga kamay na minsan mo ng tinanggihan
Andyan pa rin sila. Hindi sila nawala...

Mga munting kamay na sinasabi na "Kapit ka lang"
Kumapit ka lang sapagkat hindi ka nila bibitawan
Na kahit paulit-ulit kang bumitaw sa kanila
Paulit-ulit ka nilang itatayo at iaangat

BANGON

Sumabay ang iyong mga ngiti sa sikat ng araw
Sa pagdilat ng 'yong mga mata, nakita mo sya
Nakita mo yung bagong ikaw
Nakita mo na ang mga sugat na dala-dala mo ay unting naghilom
Mga dugo at luha na unti-unti ng natuyo

Nakita mo yung bagong ikaw
Yung ikaw na unti-unting naging matapang
Unti-unti kang naging buo
Unti-unti, dahan-dahan...

Niyakap mo yung bagong ikaw
Niyakap ka rin nya pabalik habang sinasabing
"Kinakaya mo na, wag kang bibitaw"

Nakakaya mo ng ngumiti muli
Nakakaya mo ng harapin ang bukas ng walang takot
Nakakaya mo ng bumangon
Kaya mo na.

Nakaya mo ng tanggapin na ang pag suko ay hindi pagkatalo
Nalaman mo na ang pag tanggap ay isa ring uri ng pagkapanalo
Naintindihan mo na ang pagpapatawad sa iba ay pagpapatawad din sa iyong sarili

Ngayon handa ka na...
Ang mga sugat at sakit mismo ang humubog sayo
Handa ka ng yakapin ang pagkatalo at pagka panalo
Yakapin ang saya at lungkot
Ang pag bagsak at pag bangon
Handa ka na sa panibagong sakit
Dahil alam mo na sa bawat sakit ay pagkatuto ang kalakip

Bangon na.
Bumangon ka na...

Dahil sa iyong pagbangon matatanaw mo sa dulo ang
Kanyang pangako
Na hindi sa iyak, lungkot at sakit matatapos ang lahat
Hindi dito mag tatapos ang lahat

Magtatapos ang lahat sa saya
Matatapos ito ng matapang ka
Matatapos to na nakaka tayo ka na
Matatapos to na makakalipad ka na
Dito lahat matatapos; sa nakaka ngiti ka na.

BANGON

Image credited to Chezka Laddaran

Get Back Up

English Translation

I know you have reached the point
You feel like the world is playing with you
Your destiny had also beaten you
They don't really give you a chance
to get up and to rise.

I know it's very hard to start again
Whenever you try to stand up
They will try to pull you down
And they'll say, "You're not going to make it."

You feel that the pain will slowly kill you
You will eventually become numb by it
There's nothing left but pain and suffering

You already harmed yourself
You wounded yourself
You brought blood into your own body
You cut yourself...leaving blood on your own hand

They don't know anything...
They are unaware of how much more hurt you are from within
You are more bleeding inside
You are completely broken inside

Nights when there is nothing left to do but cry
You're begging the pain to go away
You are begging with Him to end the pain because you can't take it anymore

Days without light
Days that you feel that don't exist
Days when there is no more life and
Life without a purpose.

It feels like you already lost the hope
You are completely lost in the place you once called home
You've been torn into pieces like a piece of paper
You are adrift and swept by the big waves in the ocean.

Until one day you wake up in the sunlight
You saw yourself, when the sun finally appeared
The sun that once hid you...
Light that once becomes so selfish...

In your downfall and acceptance
You saw them... You saw the people you once ignored
People you once rejected,
They're still here. They don't give up on you...

Those people will tell you "Just hold on and keep going"
Just hold on because they will not let you go,
Even if you consistently let go of them,
They will still try to help and lift you up.

As the sun begins to shine, you start embracing yourself,
When you finally accept yourself, you finally saw her...
You saw the new you... The new version of you,
You realized that you're slowly healing,
Finally, all the wounds are starting to heal.

You saw the new version of yourself,
You gain strength and wisdom,
Gradually, you become whole again,
Little by little, slowly...

You embraced the new you,
She hugged you back while saying
Keep going; You are almost there."

You can now smile again
You can face tomorrow without fear,
You can get up
You can do it.

You realize that giving up does not equal victory
You understand that accepting also signifies success
You understand that forgiving others also means forgiving yourself.

You are now prepared...
You were shaped by your own wounds and pain
You are ready to embrace defeat and victory
Embrace joy and sadness
Falling and rising
You are ready for another pain
because you know that with every pain comes with learning.

Wake up.
Get up now...
Because if you get up now,
you will see His promise in the end,
That everything will not end with crying,
sadness and pain.
This is not how you end.

Happiness wins in the end
You will end this with braveness in your heart
You will end this that you can stand on your own again
You can finally fly and dream again
Here it all ends; When you can smile and love again.

17

Pay It Forward

FLORENCIO GUINHAWA

The Guinhawa Family Scholars program, known as **Pay It Forward**, was established as part of me paying it forward to my homeland and the Filipinos. It is a payback for the deeds that many good persons provided me while I was growing up and struggling, and the chances that the Creator had given me to continue living.

My roots started in 1952. As a 7 year old, I was adopted by my mother's younger sister. I moved from Bauan, Batangas to Pasay City where I finished my elementary and secondary education. It was at Jose Abad Santos High School that I met Carlos Chan who gave me a job after graduation at age 16. Carlos later became one of my benefactors in my scholarship program.

I enrolled and graduated from college in 1970 with a BSChE, a Bachelor of Science degree in Chemical Engineering from Mapua Institute of Technology (MIT). It was a full 9 years of work, studies, and family since I got married in 1966. The marriage produced three lovely children of 2 boys and a girl.

My family and I immigrated to the United States in November, 1973. In the USA, life presented a challenge both in my personal and health life. In 1977, I underwent a 91-day Los Angeles hospital stay for colon problems, and afterwards, was followed by a divorce. I had custody of my 3 children. In 1979, we moved to Houston, Texas. After a few job changes, I settled at Bechtel Corporation in 1981 and I was a Control Systems Engineering Design Supervisor where I worked for over 39 years.

In 1999, I was discovered with Hepatitis C. In 2002-2003, I had a yearlong chemotherapy and was cured. In July 2007, I miraculously survived a major vehicular accident unscathed. And in October 2009, I was diagnosed with Stage 2 prostate cancer. A programmed radiation treatment declared me cured in August 2010. In August 2015, I was diagnosed with irregular heart beat or PVC, underwent various tests such as angiogram, EKG, ultrasound Holter monitor; and was placed on different medications. Lastly on May 2021, I underwent a trans-catheter aortic valve replacement (TAVR).

Undergoing so many trials, physical, and emotional setbacks, I still viewed my overall life as fulfilled and beautiful. Falling and bouncing back made me stronger and realized that maybe God had destined me to do something more than existing as a normal person. All my children are grown up with their own families and I had already assisted in the care of my mother and education of my immediate relatives.

The idea of the Guinhawa Family Scholarship Program at MIT started to materialize and in January 2005, I signed a Memorandum of Agreement with MIT and its president, Dr. Reynaldo Vea. In June 2008, as part of my Calabarzon educational investment, I signed a Memorandum of Agreement with Batangas State University and started the Gregorio and Esperdiona Guinhawa Scholarship in honor of my parents.

The scholarship began an exponential growth from one scholar to currently around 339 students under my scholarship program. Currently, there are a total of 8 students in school but I had graduated the following students; Mapua Institute of Technology (MIT)—75 students; Batangas State University (BSU)—59 students; University of Rizal System (URS – Morong)—93 students; Laguna State Polytechnic University (LSPU, Los Banos)—45 students; Southern Luzon State University (SLSU, Lucban)—20 students; University of the Philippines—5 students; Manuel S. Enverga University Foundation, Lucena—22 students; and various universities—12 students.

In the beginning of the scholarship program, the criteria was based primarily on academic achievements, income ability, and extracurricular activities. Mapua Institute of Technology is based on a quarter term enrollment and the students are to complete their studies in 5-quarter term years. As the applicants grew in diversity in terms of academic and income level, I decided to grant the awards based on academic achievements and financial assistance needs. An essay that illustrates how the students will be able to contribute to the club's goals of **Pay It Forward** is a requirement.

How is the program funded? It is very simple—through my paycheck and in my retirement years, my savings. What do I get in return? In January 2007, a scholars club was established by a group of students based on the teaching and the recipient's requirement to **Pay It Forward**. The club conducts and facilitates the activities of the outreach programs. The scholars club has been very active and the outreaches were completed. They include donations to the home for the elderly, orphanages, transient home for cancer patients, and home for the disabled. Going strong are the Back to School supplies drives and Brigade Eskwela.

To generate enthusiasm with the scholarship club, I sponsored seminars to further improve the personality, character, confidence of the scholars, and immersion in financial planning. RolePlayers volunteered to conduct the seminars. It was held at VMH and the Bantayog ng mga Bayani and during the pandemic so it was virtually conducted. Last face to face seminar was January 12, 2020.

Some students have fulfilled their dreams for their families. To say the least, the quality of life for the 339 graduates have been exponentially changed. Family homes had been built, repaired, and refurbished. Condos, cars, and major appliances have been purchased. Siblings have been sent to school. A majority have married and enjoy parenthood with fairly decent incomes made available by having been a graduate and passing the board examinations.

Some of them have migrated to foreign lands like myself. At present, there are alumni in the following countries: USA—2 graduates, Canada—3 graduates, Japan—3 graduates, Australia and Singapore—2 graduates, Middle East—6 graduates and Europe—3 graduates. And those who are in the Philippines continue to prosper in their own rights since everybody has a successful and well paying job. All told, the effort is well paid back and the legacy continues on.

To "pay it forward" was a dream hatched like the title of a movie. Seventeen years later, it is still a reality. I hope that my children and my alumni scholars will continue the tradition for as long as possible. I hope the scholarship program will serve as a motivation and encouragement for other Pinoys to start with their own program. If I can do it, the other Fil-Ams and Pinoys can do it better, bigger, and with more compassion.

Top photo: FCG Scholars at RolePlayers, VHM Auditorium, November 2014; Bottom photo: FCG Scholars at Golden Acres, Home for the Elderly, Tanay, Rizal, Philippines, December 2015

Top photo: FCG Scholars sy Nayon ng Kabataan, October 2012; Bottom photo: FCH Scholars at Bahay Aruga, Home for Transient Cancer Patients at PGH, January 2019

Top photo: FCG Scholars at RolePlayers with Flor (center stage) and Voltaire Gonzales, January 2019; Bottom photo: FCG Scholars at Bagong Pagasa, Calaun, Laguna, LSPU, December 2022

18

Parol

GENESIS LINGLING

Katatapos ko lamang panoorin ang paborito kong palabas sa telebisyon nang minsa'y dumungaw ako sa munting bintana ng aking silid para lumanghap ng sariwang hangin. Sa aking pagdungaw ay nasaksihan ko ang iba't ibang kumukuti-kutitap na mga ilaw na nagmumula sa mga kabahayan, kasabay ng pag-ihip ng malamig na hanging amihan na siya namang dumadampi sa buo kong katawan. Maririnig mo rin ang iba't ibang ugong ng mga sasakyan, tawanan ng mga mumunting kabataang naglalaro malapit sa aming tahanan, at ang mga nakakaindak na awiting pampasko na siyang patunay na malapit na ang araw ng kapanganakan ni Hesus.

Sa kabila ng kaligayahang aking mapagmamasdan sa kapaligiran ay siya namang kabaliktaran na namumutawi sa mukha ng dalawang bata na pilit pinipigilan ang pag-alis ng kanilang ina. Mababakas ko sa kanilang mga mukha ang kalungkutan pati na ang pangungulila. Habang pinagmamasdan ko silang mag-iina, luha'y pumatak mula sa aking mga mata.

Kasabay ng pagbalik ng isang ala-alang akala ko'y nalimot ko na.

"*Ma, wag nalang po kayong umalis. Dito nalang po kayo,*" pakiusap ko sa aking ina habang hawak ko ang magaspang niyang kamay tanda ng trabahong kanyang ginagawa araw-araw. "*Anak, gustuhin ko mang hindi umalis pero hindi pwede. Kailangan kong kumikita ng pera para may maipantustos ako sa inyong pag-aaral hanggang kolehiyo. Alam mo naman na kunti lang ang kinikita ng inyong Itay sa kanyang pangingisda,*" sagot naman ng aking ina habang pinigilan ang pag tulo ng kanyang mga luha. "*Pero Ma....*" pag angal ko sa kanya. Sa kabila ng kalungkutang nadarama ng aking ina ay nagawa pa rin nitong magbigay ng aral sa akin. "*Anak tandaan mo, ang edukasyon lamang ang tangi naming maipapamana sayo ng iyong Itay. At ang edukasyon lamang ang tanging kayaman na hindi pwedeng maagaw kahit na sino man,*" wika nito sa akin.

Matapos sabihin ito ng aking ina ay lumapit siya sa aking bunsong kapatid at kanya itong niyakap na sa mga oras na iyon ay panay ang iyak habang karga-karga ng aking ama. Pagkatapos yumakap ay isinuot niya ang isang pulseras na merong disenyo ng maliliit na mga parol at Batang Hesus sa pinaka-gitna nito sa malalambot na kamay ng aking kapatid. Sumunod namang yumakap ang aking ina sa akin na sa mga oras na iyon ay panay na ang iyak. Habang kami ay magkayakap, nagwika siya. "*Anak, pagbutihin mo ang iyong pag-aaral. Kahit ano mang manyari gusto ko na makapagtapos ka ng pag-aaral at maabot mo ang iyong pangarap sa buhay.*" Pagkatapos niyang yumakap ay kinuha niya ang isang maliit na parol sa kanyang bag at kanya itong ibinigay sa akin. At nagwikang, "*Anak, tanggapin mo ang munting parol na ito. Ito ang magsisilbi mong ilaw at gabay sa anumang daang iyong tatahakin patungo sa iyong mga pangarap.*" Sa huli ay nilapitan niya ang aking ama at nagbilin ng ilang mga mahahalagang bagay.

Sa kanyang pagtalikod ay doon ko naramdaman ang isang mainit na bagay na tumulo mula sa aking mga mata. Pinilit kong pigilan at punasan ito ngunit tila ba'y meron itong isip na nagkusa na lamang silang tumulo sa aking mga mata na parang nakakuha ng lakas mula sa iba't ibang emosyong aking nararamdaman. Bahagya akong napatakbo papunta sa kanya para pigilan siya sa kanyang pag-alis. Ngunit ako ay napigilan agad ng aking ama. Pinagmasdan ko na lamang ang unti-unting paglayo ng sasakyang sinasakyan niya hanggang sa ito ay hindi ko na makita. Habang nakatingin parin sa direksiyon kung saan nagtungo ang sasakyang sinasakyan niya ay nagwika at sinambit ko na lamang ang mga salitang nagsilbing pangako ko sa aking sarili, *"Ma, kahit na malayo ka man sa amin ay mananatili ka paring kasakasama namin. Dahil ang parol na ito ang magsisilbing ikaw. Ang magsisilbing ilaw at gabay ko tungo sa aking pangarap na maging isang magaling na guro. Ang bawat ilaw ng parol na ito ay ang magsisilbi kong lakas at determinasyon tungo sa aking pangarap. At sa iyong pag-uwi ay ibabalik ko ang parol na ito kasama ng aking naabot na pangarap."*

Sa pagdaan ng panahon ay pinagbutihan ko ang aking pag-aaral. Nagpursige akong matutunan ang lahat ng mga aralin sa paaralan. Kahit na may mga balakid na bigla nalang dumarating sa aking buhay. Hinding hindi ako papatinag dito. Bagkus ay magiging mas determinado ako sa aking pag-aaral. Sobrang saya ng aking ama sa pinapakita kong pagpupursige. Kaya sa aking pagtatapos sa Sekondarya ay nakuha ko ang ikalimang pinakamataas na karangalan. Labis ang kasiyahang nadama ng aking mga magulang lalong lalo na ang aking ina na kasalukuyang nagtatrabaho noon sa Manila.

Sa aking pagtatagumpay sa sekondarya ay nagbukas muli ang isang pinto sa aking buhay. Ito ay dahil sa naging iskolar ako sa isang prestihiyosong paaralan sa Calbayog City, ang Northwest Samar State University.

Ang naturang scholarship program ay ang ESGP-PA o ang Expanded Students' Grant-in-Aid Program for Poverty Alleviation ng 4P's. Na siyang tumulong sa akin upang matustusan ang aking pag-aaral sa kolehiyo. Dito kinuha ko ang kursong Bachelor of Secondary Education major in Biological Science. Sa tulong ng ESGP-PA ay nagkaroon ako ng ibat ibang mga opporturnidad sa aking pag-aaral. Una ay ang pagiging kalahok ko sa isang pambansang patilampak sa pagsulat ng sanaysay na ginanap sa Baguio City noong Setyembre 26, 2016. At dahil na rin sa aking pagiging iskolar ay hindi na masyadong namomroblema ang aking mga magulang sa pantustus ko sa mga bayarin sa paaralan. Sa katunayan ay mas nakatulong pa ako sa kanila. Sa aking apat na taon ng pag-aaral sa kolehiyo ay hindi maiiwasang may mga balakid at pagsubok na dumating sa aking buhay. May mga araw at gabing umiiyak at nagtatago nalang ako sa sulok ng aking silid dahil sa pagod at tindi ng stress na aking nararamdaman. Pero nagawa ko paring lampasan ang lahat ng iyon.

Sa araw ng aking pagtatapos sa kolehiyo ay masayang masaya ako. Ito kasi ang araw na makakasama ko na ang aking mga magulang sa pag-akyat sa entablado habang kinukuha ang minimithi kong diploma. Ngunit sa araw naring iyon ay tumawag ang aking ina sa akin at sinabing hindi niya magagawang makarating sa araw ng aking pagtatapos kasi hindi siya pinayagan ng kanyang amo na makauwi. Dahil sa balitang aking narinig, ako ay bahagyang nalungkot dahil hindi ko makikita ang kasiyahan at mga ngiting mamumutawi sana sa kanyang mukha. Ngunit sa kabila ng balitang aking natanggap ay pinilit ko paring maging masaya dahil kasama ko naman ang aking suportadong ama at kapatid sa entablado.

Ilang lingo matapos ang aking pagtatapos ay doon ko naramdaman ang pagkatakot. Ako ay naguguluhan at hindi ko alam ang gagawin kong ako ba ay magtatrabaho para makatulong na sa aking mga magulang o magpopokus muna ako sa aking pagrereview para sa nalalapit na board exam. Habang ako ay nasa aking munting silid ay pinagmasdan ko ang munting parol na bigay sa akin ng aking ina kasabay ng pagtitimbang ng mga bagay bagay. Sa aking pag-iisip ay napagdesisyonan kong magpokus nalang muna sa aking rereview para sa parating na board exam dahil kung sakaling makapasa ako ay wala na akong poproblemahin pa. Diretso na ang aking pagtatrabaho.

Sa aking pagrereview sa board exam ay hindi ko maiwasang maramdaman ang pagod at stress. Ngunit hindi ako nagpatinag dito. Bagkus nagpursige ako sa aking pag-aaral. Sa katunayan umaabot pa ako ng madaling araw kakabasa at kakaunawa ng lahat ng mga aralin na dapat kong pag-aaralan. Kasabay na rin ang pagtitiwala sa aking sarili at sa Panginoong Lumikha. Hanggang sa dumating na nga ang mismong araw ng pagsusulit. Setyembre 30, 2018. Dito ko ibinuhos ang lahat ng aking makakaya para sa aking pangarap. Hindi ako nagpadala sa kaba at takot. Bagkus akin itong ginamit para mapalalim at mapatatag ko pa ang aking paniniwala sa Diyos. Hindi rin nawala sa aking isip ang parol na binigay sa akin ng aking ina na siyang nagpapalakas ng aking loob at determinasyon. Sa katunayan ay akin itong isinabit malapit kay Hesus bago ako umalis papuntang Tacloban para sa pagsusulit. Lumipas ang araw na iyon na puro pagsasagot at paguunawa sa mga katangunan ang aking ginawa. Pagkalabas ko sa paaralan na aking pinagexaman ay pumunta agad ako kasama ng aking mga kaibigan sa simbahan upang magpasalamat sa Diyos kasabay ang pangakong makakapasa ako.

Sa aking paghihintay sa magiging resulta ng pagsusulit ay hindi mawala sa aking isipan ang pagkatakot, pagduda at mga pangamba kung sakaling hindi ako makapasa. Ang ginawa ko para maibsan ang bigat na aking nararamdaman ay palagi nalang akong nagdadasal sa Diyos at tinitingnan ang parol na para bang kumukuha ako ng lakas sa tuwing makakaramdam ako kaba at pagdududa. Hindi ako nawalan ng pag-asa na makapasa. At sa pagdating ng araw ng paglabas ng resulta ng pagsusulit ay nagkulong lang ako sa aking kwarto habang nagdadasal. Nasa tabi ko rin ang parol na bigay ng aking in ana para bang nagbibigay ito ng liwanag at pag-asang makakamit ko ang tagumpay. Ika walo noon ng gabi ay nakatanggap ako ng isang tawag mula sa aking ina.

"Anak, masayang masaya ako sa naabot mo ngayon," wika niya.

"HUH? Bakit po inay?" sagot ko ng may pagtataka.

"Anak, hindi mo ba alam? Nak nakapasa sa board exam. Ngayon ay isa kanang ganap na "guro," wika niya sa kanyang napakasayang boses.

"Totoo po ba yan inay?" sagot ko naman sa kanya.

"Oo anak. Totoong-totoo. Tiningnan kasi ng amo kung babae ang lumabas na resulta ng pagsusulit at kanya itong pinakita sa akin na nadun ang iyong pangalan," pagpapaliwanag niya.

At napalundag ako sa aking narinig.

Mula sa aking pagmumuni-muni at pagbabaliktanaw sa nakaraan, ako ay nakaramdam ng isang mainit na yakap kasabay ng isang malambing na boses na nagsasabing, "Maligayang Pasko, aking Anak." At napagtanto kong nasa likod ko na pala ang aking ina.

"Anak, may tinatanaw kaba sa iyong bintana? Tila ba'y ang lungkot ng iyong mukha?" wika ng aking ina.

"Wala po Inay, meron lamang akong iniisip. Halika na at kumain na tayo ng Noche Buena. Nananabik na akong makita ang iyong regalo sa akin," pagaaya ko sa kanya.

Lantern

English Translation

I had just finished watching my favorite television show when I looked out the small window of my room to breathe fresh air. When I looked, I witnessed various flickering lights coming from the houses of our neighbors. At the same time, the cold north wind blows, which in turn touches my whole body whispering to me something. You will also hear the different hums of cars, laughter of young children playing near our house, and the haunting Christmas carols that are a proof of the day that Jesus' birth is near.

Despite the happiness that I could observe in the environment, it was the opposite that appeared on the faces of the two children who were trying to prevent their mother from leaving. I can trace the sadness and longing on their faces. As I watched them, tears fell from my eyes—along with the return of a memory I thought I had forgotten.

"Mom, don't leave. Stay here," I begged my mother as I held her rough hands, a reminder of the work she does every day. *"Son, I would like not to leave but I can't. I need to earn money so that I can pay for your education until college. You know that your father only earns a little from his fishing,"* my mother replied while holding back her tears. *"But Ma...."* I whined at her.

Despite the sadness my mother felt, she still managed to teach me a lesson. *"Son, remember, education is the only thing that your father can bequeath to you. And education is the only wealth that cannot be taken away by anyone,"* she said to me.

After my mother said this, she came to my younger brother and hugged him, who at that time was constantly crying while being carried by my father. After hugging him she put on a bracelet with a design of small lanterns and Baby Jesus in the very center of it, on my brother's soft hands. Next, my mother hugged me, who at that time was crying constantly. While we were hugging, she said. *"Son, improve your studies. No matter what happens, I want you to graduate and achieve your dreams in life."*

After hugging, she took a small lantern from her bag and gave it to me. And said, *"Son, accept this little lantern. This will serve as your light and guide in any road you will take towards achieving your dreams."* In the end, she approached my father and entrusted some important things.

As she turned away, I felt something warm drip from my eyes. I tried to wipe it but it seemed to have a mind of its own. A burst of emotions spreads within me. I wanted to run and stop her from leaving. But my father held my hand. I had no choice but to watch her at the window of the car as they left. I was left telling myself: *"Ma, even if you are away from us, you will always be with us. This lantern will serve as your presence. The one who will serve as my light and guide towards my dream of becoming a good teacher. Each light of this lantern will serve as my strength and determination in achieving my dreams. And when you come home, I will return this lantern with my achieved dreams."*

As time went by, I improved my studies. I persisted in learning all the lessons in school. Even though there were obstacles that suddenly came in my life. I will never budge from this. But I will be more determined in my studies. My father was very happy with my persistence.

So, when I graduated from high school, I got the fifth highest honor. My parents were very happy, especially my mother who was currently working in Manila.

With my success in secondary school, a door opened again in my life. This is because I became a scholar in a prestigious school in Calbayog City, the Northwest Samar State University. The scholarship program is the ESGP-PA or the Expanded Students' Grant-in-Aid Program for Poverty Alleviation of the 4P's and this scholarship helped me to finance my college education. Here, I took the course Bachelor of Secondary Education major in Biological Science. With the help of ESGP-PA I had various opportunities in my studies. First is my participation in a national essay writing competition held in Baguio City on September 26, 2016. And also because of my scholarship, my parents didn't have too much of a problem with my school fees. In fact, I helped them even more. During my four years of college studies, it was inevitable that obstacles and trials came into my life. There were days and nights where I cried and hid in the corner of my room because of the fatigue and intensity of the stress I felt. But I still managed to overcome all that.

On the day of my college graduation, I was very happy. This is the day that I will be able to join my parents in going up on the stage while getting my dream diploma. But that day, my mother called me and said that she won't be able to make it to the day of my graduation because her boss wouldn't let her go. I was saddened by the news I'd heard, since I wouldn't be able to see the happiness and smiles that would have appeared on her face. But despite the news I've received, I still tried to smile and be happy because I was with my supportive father and sister on stage.

A few weeks after my graduation, I felt fear. I'm confused and I don't know what to do—will I work to help my parents or will I focus first on my review for the upcoming board exam? While I was in my small room, I looked at the little lantern that my mother gave me while weighing things. In my mind, I decided to focus first on my review for the upcoming board exam, because if I pass, I won't have any more problems. I'd work straight away.

During my review for the board exam, I couldn't help but feel tired and stressed. But I didn't let it get to me. Instead, I persevered in my studies. In fact, I studied into the early hours of the morning, reading and understanding all the lessons I needed to study. All the while, trusting myself and the Lord Creator. The actual exam day came. September 30, 2018. This is where I poured everything I could into achieving my dream of becoming a teacher. I did not show any signs of fear and anxiety. Rather, I used it to deepen and strengthen my faith in God. I also did not forget the lantern that my mother gave me which strengthened my courage and determination. In fact, I hung it near the altar before I left for Tacloban for the exam. A day went by and I just only answered and understood the questions from the exam. At exactly five o'clock in the afternoon, I finished my exam and got out of the school. I immediately went with my friends to the church to thank God while assuring myself that I would pass.

While I was waiting for the result of the exam—fear, doubts and apprehensions in case I could not pass—didn't disappear in my mind. To ease the weight of what I was feeling, I prayed to God and looked at the lantern as if I was getting strength every time I felt nervous and doubtful. I never lost hope of passing. And when the day of the exam result came, I just locked myself in my room while praying. I also have the lantern next to me as if it gives light and hope that I will achieve success.

At eight o'clock in the evening, I received a call from my mother. *"Son, I am very happy with what you have achieved today,"* she said. *"HUH? Why mother?"* I answered with surprise.

"Son, don't you know? You passed the board exam. Now, you are a true master," she said in her very happy voice.

"Is that true mother?" I answered him.

"Yes son. Very true. The boss was checking the test results and she showed me that your name was there." she explained.

I jumped at what I heard. I felt a warm embrace and I looked back. A soft voice said, *"Merry Christmas, my Son."*

I realized that my mother was behind me, *"Son, are you looking at something from your window? Why does your face look sad?"* my mother said.

"No Mom, I'm just thinking about something. Come and let's eat Noche Buena. I can't wait to see your gift for me," I said to make her feel welcomed back.

Top photo: Conquering LET Board Exam; Bottom left photo: Genesis and his mother on Graduation Day; Bottom right photo: Genesis Lingling's teaching photo

19

Mangarap Ka

CHEZKA LADDARAN

Ang sabi nila kapag mahirap ka ay wala kang pangarap
Pinanganak kang mahirap kung kaya't mamatay kang mahirap
Pero mali, huwag mong hayaan na diktahan ka ng iba
Huwag kang maniwala sa sinasabi nila

Basta, bata mangarap ka nang malalim
Yung pangarap na hindi kayang sukatin ng tingin
Yun pangarap na hindi maipaliwanag ng damdamin
Yung pangarap na hindi mananakaw ng sino man sa amin.

Mangarap ka nang malalim
Ngunit walang bahid ng sakim
Yung may puso at damdamin
Yung may matinding hangarin

Basta bata ipangako mo mangangarap ka
Hindi lang maging mabait pati na rin maging mabuti
Kung paano maging patas at hindi daanin sa dahas
Kung paano lumaban at huwag umatras

MANGARAP KA

Susubukin ka nang tadhana
Hahamunin ka ng kapalaran
Pilitin mong mapunta sa tamang daan
Huwag kang magpapadala sa kasamaan

At pag sapit nang araw
Isang pangarap ang mangingibabaw
Kaya huwag kang bibitaw
Dahil sigurado ikaw ay masisilaw
Sa mga pangako Nyang magandang araw

Basta mangarap ka nang mahaba
Isantabi mo ang takot sa kanila
Mangarap ka
Sasamahan ka Nya
Sasamahan kita

Just Dream

English Translation

They say when you are born poor, it means you don't have a dream
You were born poor, and you will die poor
But they are wrong, don't let other people dictate you
You shouldn't believe what they say

Youth, you should have deep dreams
Dreams that you cannot measure with your eyes
Dreams that no one can explain
Dreams that no one can take away from you.

Just dream deeply
but without hate and greedy
and be sure to have a pure heart and feelings
and a strong desire to make it.

Promise me you'll dream
Not just to be kind, but also to be good
Dream also to be fair and not to betray others
how to fight and never give up.

Life will challenge you
Your fate will put you to the test
Try to be on the right path
And don't let evil persuade you.

And when the right time comes
Your dream will come true
So, keep on going and dreaming
Because better days are coming
And His promises will be fulfilled

Just dream deeply
Set aside your worries and fears

MANGARAP KA

Just keep dreaming
The Lord will guide you.
Because I will be with you

20

Never Heard Of Such A Thing: How I Became An International Storyteller

JAY MENES

WE USED TO LIVE in the neighborhood of Punta, Sta. Ana, Manila, a compound less than a kilometer from the Pasig River, wherein reading materials are not available when you want to read something. Public libraries are a rare gem in the city. I love watching and mimicking the characters of my favorite cartoon series, which includes Popeye, Carebears, Thundercats, and Astroboy.

I'd always want to grab a comic book or magazine resembling it.

During my childhood, I could rent anything with a drawing and story in our favorite *sari-sari* store. Liwayway magazine's comic strips are the best for me, most especially *The Kenkoy* by Anthony "Tony" Velasquez and *Spice of Life* by Larry Alcala in the Weekend Magazine of Daily Express. To continue with this, I have to find ways to make money.

I sold sweet street snacks that my mother cooked, like banana-q, kamote-q, and turon. She would give me coins so I could return to my favorite *sari-sari* store and rent the *Pilipino Komiks, Funny Komiks*. Twice a week, I would fetch water to fill the big container of our Muslim renter, and she will pay me a more considerable amount. It goes like this most of the time; however, I need help buying the comic books I like.

My desire to own a book was a dream for me until I finished college. I can only buy and collect books when I am already working and earning a good amount of money. *How can I have a book when I would rather buy food instead?* The answer is no, I cannot buy and collect books, because I allotted my salary to pay the bills, food, and support for my family members.

After working in a Malaysian bank for seven years, I decided to resign and pursue something else. I went into performing arts, you know, the likes of acting, hosting, singing with dancing, teaching, and a party talent supplier.

I have a friend that enjoys reading, and they have the money to buy books. She would share her excitement and her takeaways with me. So one day, she gave me a gift, a book entitled *The Greatest Salesman in the World* by Og Mandino. Then, it started to spark the light of my childhood hobby of reading, and now I own a book. I read the book for one week, and after that, I am looking for another one to read. "Never feel shame for trying and failing, for he who has never failed is he who has never tried." This line from Mandino's book struck me to keep on trying. I realized then I have to make it a point to set aside an amount to buy one book every month. At first, it was hard to do that; however, the next thing I was always visiting the bookstore to find the book I would buy.

The day came when I could buy a beautiful book with the same theme as the gifted one. Since then, I have been a frequent visitor to different bookstores in Metro Manila to find what interests me. As I kept on doing this, I was happy to be surrounded by people that are into arts and promoting culture. I've tried attending workshops that teach hosting as a clown, how to do magic tricks, puppetry, ventriloquism, miming, voice lessons, playing percussion instruments, musical theatre, stage acting, modern jazz, hip-hop, directing, and eventually, storytelling. All in the name of trying, inspired by Og Mandinos' quotation.

I turn into a person who engages in performing on stage. And because I wanted to explore other art forms, I attended a storytelling workshop in Museo Pambata, Manila with my wife, who is a public school teacheryou mu in 2002. The facilitator taught us how to read a book in an interactive manner. So, I tried this, and eventually, I became good at it. The group got me as their regular story reader for the different events sponsored by the Book Publishers. I could travel around Metro Manila and out of town with schools and NGO invitations. Apparently, after two years with them, I decided to be with one publisher, Adarna House Publishing. With them, I worked as a workshop facilitator and an interactive story reader in full swing. The company was able to let me travel around the archipelago. And the perks of working with the publishers are that I no longer buy books, because they give me the newly published books for free, or sometimes I can arrange the payment of my service into books instead.

It was 2004 when I met an International Storyteller for the very first time. It is her homecoming to the Philippines after so many years. Dianne de las Casas is a Filipino-American and an award-winning author. She conducted a workshop for Storytellers in the house of our group leader. It was raining hard that night, but I managed to be present. In the seminar, I saw her passion and generosity. After finishing the talk, she walked toward me and handed me a photocopy of *How to Market Yourself as a Storyteller*. I kept it and read it almost every day.

Our group had a performance at Shangri-La Plaza Mall and Dianne was called up and performed on the main stage. Now, for the first time, I witnessed how a Storyteller performs; she is telling the story, not reading any book. I was amazed to watch her performance. The reason is that our group holds a book, while Dianne is telling the story orally by memory. Since that day, it began my conscious effort to learn and to do an in-depth study about her storytelling performance.

In 2008, Dianne returned to the Philippines, and we met again. I shared with her how that copy helped me to get more bookings. I traveled to most parts of the Philippines doing story reading and facilitating workshops.

Due to my research, I learned that there is a yearly gathering of International Storytellers in Singapore. I plan to go there, but my funds still need to be released. One morning while I was doing my part-time job as a Sales Manager at a company that buys and sells cars, I was able to make a sale that day. The commission allowed me to pay for the workshop fees and airfare and book at a backpackers' inn. I attended the Singapore International Storytelling Festival in 2008. There were very few Filipinos in attendance.

In July 2009, I went to Museo Pambata as per the invitation of the Executive Director to participate in the Storytelling Workshop done by South African storyteller, Gcina Mhlophe-Becker. In her workshop, she incorporated the storytelling performance. It was a fantastic spectacle of her talent.

For the third time, Dianne and I met in 2010, and it was an excellent rendezvous because I am beginning to understand what it is to be a Storyteller, that in my mind, I want to be doing what she is doing, which is performing stories around the world.

In February 2011, Gcina was in the Philippines to do her seminar workshop at the Museo Pambata. After her performance, the Philippines Ambassador of the Embassy of the Republic of South Africa talked to me and said, "You must perform the next time." This was the encouragement I needed to go further, and this time I was convinced I will be a Storyteller telling and performing Filipino stories to the world.

Next month later, I formed the storytelling group—Storyhouse Philippines with the approval of Dianne de las Casas. She inspired me to go on, do the telling, and let the stories flow inside of me. I decided to go to Singapore again to attend the International Storytelling Festival in September. I watched all of the Storytellers with so much gusto and enthusiasm. While in my seat, I imagine that one of these days, I will be on that stage performing our well-loved Filipino folktales. On the last day of the conference, it seals the deal that I am a Storyteller from the Philippines. The inspirations and motivations of Dianne and Gcina made me desire to be an International Storyteller.

Do you still remember the Yahoo groups? Luckily, when I received the email, I expressed an interest in joining the call to participate as one of the Guest Performers of the Talk Story Festival by Jeff Gere of Hawaii, U.S.A.

He said in the email, "I've gotten a huge response, some really good national tellers, but none are from the Philippines—I'd like to have you visit and inform us about the storytelling world you know."

The next hurdle for Filipinos in the Philippines is the U.S. visa! I am working at that time as an Outbound Call Center Agent. My immediate superior used to work in the U.S. Embassy in the Philippines as Visa Assistant. I got some tips and tricks from him; it made me stronger than before going through this obstacle. I applied for a visa is online, and then I paid the fees at the bank. After that, I emailed the receipt, booked the interview appointment date, and lastly prepared the documents (almost bringing the cabinet, not literally) and went to the embassy for the interview. During my time with the Consular Officer, it took me more or less than five minutes to hear the sentence, "Your visa is approved!" Could you imagine how I felt that day? I was so delighted that day, that after I heard it, I turned my back and I pumped my fist, saying a loud "Yes!" inside myself.

Fortunately, I reached Hawaii—my first stint overseas. Dianne also resided there when she was still young, and eventually, I did some performances and toured around the island. I performed at the Filipino Community Center (FilCom Center) courtesy of Ms. Rose Churma. Also, I had a Skype interview with Kababayan Today host Janelle So in Los Angeles.

The next international gig was in Singapore in 2014. I performed at my wife's school and at the school of my friend who is the principal, while I participated at the SISF and joined in at their story swap. I already made friends with the Singapore storytellers, Sheila Wee and Kamini Ramachandran this time.

In 2015, Iran International Storytelling Festival was looking for participants, and they sent an invitation through email and social media so that they could get more people to join. I motivated myself to participate in this event, though in my head I asked myself, "Is it dangerous in Iran? What will happen if I will not be able to return alive? Am I going to encounter a terrorist?" I was successfully chosen by the organizer to go to Iran but not just to Tehran (the city capital); we went to the province of Kermanshah. It is located in the west of Iran and has a dominant Kurdish population. I loved the rich collection of natural and historical attractions. When I arrived, it was sunny, but the temperature was negative, 7 degrees. The following days are changing because it is frigid. Who would have thought that Iran is so chilly?

After three days of the festival, I was declared the winner. I can't believe that our audience, the organizer, and the committee would love and enjoy my story. The performances I did with my translator are how I usually perform. As a performer, you must feel what the audience is feeling and try to be in tune with them. When I did the folk story *Pilandok and the Crocodiles*, I incorporated the song, "We Will Rock You" by Queen. I changed the lyrics to "we will, we will eat you," accompanied by the hand gesture of the mouth of the crocodile while inviting everyone in the audience to sing and gesture. I feel like a rockstar having a concert. It was a blast!

Being in Iran made me feel very wrong about the news, gossip, and captions about what was there. Don't judge a book by its cover now by its headlines. The festival seems like I attended the Oscar Awards Night for Storytellers or Venice Film Festival because all of us were like superstars, or I should say super storytellers. I love being with Iranians; they are like my people in the Philippines. Friendly, warm, and hospitable, and also fond of singing and dancing. Actually, in 2018 they invited me again as a Jury for the International Storytellers showcase.

The same year, I went to the Bay Area Storytelling Festival in Orinda, California, International Festival

Morocco Tales in Rabat, and Sharjah International Narrator Forum. It goes on and on and on, telling Filipino stories to the world. I wish many would follow suit so that our *kababayans* and other nationalities would know while listening to our wonderful folktales.

There is a quote that says you will need to read and get to know a lot of stories to find the stories you want to tell. Most storytellers approximate that they read 100 stories to find the one they like. Storytellers will tell you that often you don't see the story, but the story finds you. In my case, I chose stories that imply adventure, entail fun in life, being different is not different, and we can always win if we work together.

The legacy they bestowed upon me will continue to sparkle as I ignite this brilliant idea in my mind, and my heart towards sharing Filipino stories with more countries. To date, I am so glad to meet other International Storytellers excitedly sharing stories from their countries. We die only once. Why not make history? Unto the next journey of reading, of telling Filipino stories, and sharing our magnificent culture to the world.

Top left photo: Jay Menes professional photo; Top right photo: Jay performing at the Iranian Storytelling Festival; Bottom left photo: Jay at the 19th Sharjah International Narrators Forum; Bottom right photo: Jay greeting his audience hello

21

A Personal Statement

MARIE SALAZAR

When I was a young girl, I remember being beside my grandmother who was holding a mortar and pestle, grinding and mixing nuts with other ingredients. She would wrap it in a leaf to make a bolus which she chewed. She seemed to enjoy it while telling stories about World War II. What caught my attention were her teeth. They were reddish brown. I wondered what the rest of the inside of her mouth looked like. I was intrigued by this and began to read books and researched what was the gum she was chewing and its effects on her teeth. This started my journey and interest in dentistry.

My path to becoming a dentist has been quite the journey. During my second year of dental school, at 19, I got pregnant and I got married. My parents were understandably shocked and heart-broken, deciding not to let me finish my education. This did not deter me from pursuing what I love to do. I was still determined to become a dentist. My passion to serve, collaborate, to be socially involved in uplifting oral health, and inclination to art and beauty– propelled my desire to continue. I used this passion as a driving force to do everything I could possibly do to reach my goal in life and finish dental school.

At that time, there was no educational financial assistance in the Philippines. With no support from my parents, my husband helped in financing my education. It was not easy. We still had to sacrifice to find ways to make ends meet with the added expense of my schooling. I sold purses, jeans, and even firecrackers to be able to support my clinical expenses. I also missed being with my first daughter and can only see her once a week. My heart broke every time she cried when I had to leave for school again. These challenges fueled me to excel and become more determined to fight the odds. I balanced being a wife, mother, and dental student. My GPA was affected by these challenges. In one class, my professor caught me dozing off from lack of sleep, taking care of the baby, and studying at night. She gave me a failing mark on the subject, Fixed Prosthodontics. I had to take it again during the summer. I took it as a positive reinforcement and a blessing in disguise. The mentor during the summer was more detailed and I was able to learn more on the clinical side. I always remembered what my grandmother taught me—that sacrifice will lead to success.

After graduating from dental school in 1992 at 24 years old, I set up a small private practice in the province where I grew up, province South of Luzon. I honed my skills by furthering my education, attending preceptorship, training, and workshops locally and internationally. Service has been instilled in me at an early age. My grandfather was a mayor of a small island in the Philippines. It was just an ordinary day seeing people with children lined up at my grandfather's doorstep to ask for assistance, food, clothing, medicine, and shelter were the major concerns. This was where I learned empathy. My father was a medical doctor who gave free consultation to the farmers and other underprivileged and malnourished residents. We always had fresh vegetables, eggs, sometimes meat on the table as their way of paying back my father.

Giving back to the community was therefore a priority for me. I volunteered for over 10 years to do oral exams to thousands of students from the elementary school and high school I attended. This experience trained me in managing children and learned numerous ways on how to gain their trust. Majority of the children hesitated in participating or even just going inside the school's clinic because of the fear they had for people in white coats. They equated them with getting injections. To remove this stigma, I started oral health education in classrooms using colorful puppets demonstrating how to brush properly, colorful cartoon stories about tooth decay, and I depicted myself as the heroine in the fight against tooth decay and pain. I took off the lab coat and wore bright colorful dresses for children to associate good memories about oral health class. These created an impact on the changes in their behavior. The children became excited for their oral exam. A report was sent to all the parents giving emphasis on oral prophylaxis and pit and fissure sealants. The school administration noted a 60% decline in absenteeism due to toothache.

These children were my first patients in my private practice. A few of them even pursued dentistry and became dentists themselves, including my own daughter. My private practice grew from doing general dentistry and later expanding to Orthodontics, Periodontology, and Implant Dentistry. I became involved in corporate dental practice, providing services to employees and their families in companies like Wyeth and Bayer. One incident that led me to corporate dentistry was a patient who needed denture work. He asked me if I could fit him with dentures and he would pay me back on his first paycheck when he gets a job. This taught me the importance of my career which gave me a feeling of satisfaction having to make a difference in the lives of others.

I became very involved in community outreach by soliciting funds from companies and elected officials and creating activities for fundraising. I continued to do oral education until 2019 reaching out to communities with no access to dental services. Joining the Philippine Dental Association early on in my career harnessed my leadership skills. In May of 2019, I was awarded Most Outstanding Chapter President Nationwide from the Philippine Dental Association. The practice model I did in school was adapted to outreach programs aimed to promote oral health in areas that were geographically isolated and disadvantaged in terms of location, water supply, and deprived access for medical and dental needs. Malnourished children with poor oral hygiene due to lack of dental supplies caught my attention. Adults also had widespread periodontal diseases. I needed to act.

I spearheaded fundraising campaigns like "Golf for a Cause" and Blockbuster movie showings to earn funds to fund projects with collaborations with the government, other dentists, teachers, and other non-government organizations. The projects were to promote oral health education, dental checkups, remote restorations, pit and fissure sealants, proper hand washing, nutrition counseling, and feeding programs. My responsibilities to my profession increased. I got involved in organizing Continuing Education for 800 local dentists quarterly. One of which was a conference I spearheaded, "Laguna Goes to Britain," where 27 Filipino delegates went to London, exposing them to technologies, practices, and collaboration with foreign counterparts. This kept them abreast with latest technologies with everyone participating in Dentinal Tubules Congress,

British Dental Show, and hands-on training in C-Fast Cosmetics.

In 2012, my youngest daughter moved to Texas, USA. I deferred moving with her permanently due to my responsibilities in the community outreach and my thriving dental practice in the Philippines. In October 2019, I finally moved here to the U.S. permanently. The following year, COVID hit the world, and the dental practice as everything else, was affected. I decided to take a different career path by studying Medical Coding and Medical Assisting at Houston Community College. I also enrolled in English as a Second Language to improve my communication skills and adapt to American verbiage.

Change is a constant force and leaving my comfort zone was scary. Moving here to the U.S., I experienced challenges being an immigrant. I learned humility and acceptance. I adapted to the new and different work environments and learned how to interact with people with diverse backgrounds. One of the challenges for me is not having a network of people who could vouch for my experiences and not having a license to even work as a dental assistant. To overcome that, I took review classes, took the Dental Assisting National Board exam, and passed to become a certified Orthodontic Assistant. I finally acquired my license as a Registered Dental Assistant (RDA) here in Texas. I also joined Cloud Dentistry, an app that lists part-time jobs in the field. In the first months, even though I was frustrated because nobody hired me citing my lack of experience working here in the U.S., I did not give up. Instead, I furthered my education through online training and learned different software like Open Dental, Dentrix, Eagle Soft and others so I can bolster my resume.

Finally, a Filipino-African dentist hired me to work part time as an RDA. I worked hard and applied the same work ethics I always have. I became dependable and my rating in the Cloud Dentistry app increased and my bookings increased not only in Houston, but I got work as far as Port Arthur and Orange in Texas. The traveling aspect was a bonus. I was able to navigate the extensive freeway of Texas from north to south, east and west, as well as enjoying the scenery. As I worked, I felt again the same satisfaction and a sense of fulfillment in my life that I used to have. I noticed there were patients who would request me to assist the doctor. Little by little, I am learning a lot, like the workflows for each day, how to break the room, being comfortable and proficient in using the different software programs for charting. I am also learning the value of teamwork with other assistants, communicating with patients, setting appointments, and managing insurance verification. I learned to use iTero, 3D printing, and automated impression materials. These are modern equipment with more predictable results by using technologies that could greatly improve analysis and minimize mistakes. All these again fueled my desire to seek further education and get a license to practice here in the U.S. and get back to my original love for dentistry.

With 25 years of experience as a foreign dentist, I believe I still have a lot to explore in terms of improving my clinical skills, reviving my purpose to share my management and entrepreneurial skills, correcting, and applying new knowledge to improve and give a better quality of treatment, and avoiding mistakes made in my past dental practice while adapting U.S. standards. In the next five years I see myself as a practicing dentist in the U.S., involved in teaching and research. In the 2008 movie, "The Curious Case of Benjamin Button" Button says, "For what it's worth... It's never too late to be whoever you want to be. There is no time limit. Start whenever you want. You can change or stay the same. We can make the best or the worst of it." Being a dentist is not just a career for me, it is my life's calling. I answered it once. It is calling me again.

22

balikbayan box

AL AGUILAR

*Context is what steadies
a third eye's
aim*

A cardboard cauldron
of familial bonds,
political ramifications,
safety magic, and
funneled
salvation.

History is saw-toothed
in how it separates
generations.
But you can seal
your heart
in a box
until your heart is
simultaneously both
alive

and
dead.

Heritage can collapse
and is left
wanting
once the box
is
opened.

"How much is
postage
to send
non-perishable
Kapwa?"

Context can't fill
in where loss resides
but it can deliver
us out of
absence

23

Mapping Love and Longing in Chicago

VICTOR BARNUEVO VELASCO

THE VOICE ON THE other end started to panic when I informed her that our men would be at her place in less than fifteen minutes. "Can't they delay their arrival?" she pleaded. "I need to go to the grocery and buy five pounds of apples." I said that might not be possible as they still had half of Chicago in their route. "I really need to fill up the box, I thought I had enough." Panic turned into desperation. "Hold on *po*," I started to panic, too, "are you buying apples to send back to the Philippines in the *balikbayan* box?" She said yes. "*Ay naku*," I held off laughing, "they will arrive in Manila as apple juice." At first she thought I was teasing her. But after I insisted the transit would take more than a month, if not two, she agreed that we would pick up her box in the next schedule, to give her time to gather items she could send to family back home.

Home was a polar magnet that directed many driveways in Chicago to a group of islands in the Pacific. Whether the household had settled in the Windy City for less than a year or for five decades, they always referred to the Philippines as home. They say, "I like to send a *balikbayan* box *home*."

In Summer of 2002, after four years of working in information technology that offered comfort and security, I got laid off. By then I had years of paying rent and utilities in dollars, buying groceries in bulks, and had my own car. The sudden switch from a cozy job to an uncertain situation was unnerving. It was my first time being jobless involuntarily. My entire family was in the Philippines, and I had to keep my situation to myself. I thought that informing them would only give them unnecessary worry. But keeping the façade of doing well also meant that I had to continue supporting them by sending money regularly, even as I had to dip into my savings while looking for new work. By then Y2K jobs had long been over, Web 1.0 was imploding, and 9/11 displaced thousands of workers I had to compete with in a very limited job market.

After two months of searching for a corporate role, my savings started to deplete. I took a minimum-wage job with a Filipino-owned company. That was then I discovered a hidden Chicago. The company processed remittances from Filipino immigrants to their families back home. They also shipped *balikbayan* boxes to the Philippines. *Balikbayan,* literally returning home, were care packages of anything imaginable that could fill a corrugated box. Weight limit on the box was virtually non-existent, which meant anyone could send anything, from bathroom tissue to toilet bowl.

I had availed of this service myself. I learned from friends that I could fill a big box over several weeks, scouring discount sales on weekends, adding more items during salary day, until the box could hardly be closed. I also learned from them that shoes would best be removed from their original boxes, then stuffed with several rolled socks; shirts and jeans could be folded many times over; air-filled plastic packages needed to be deflated—all to maximize space and be able to add just one more other item.

For most immigrants and overseas Filipino workers, these boxes were surrogate bodies. Unable to visit home for long periods, they sent back instead the scents, tastes, colors, and textures of America. Never mind that some of the items were cheaper back home, never mind that sometimes the items they were sending were made back home, proving that *balikbayan* truly meant returning to their place or origin.

My work had three main tasks. The first task was to receive requests for pickup of the boxes. With that, I had to gather the details about the sender: where the box was going, how many boxes would be sent, and the address where they would be picked up. During this time, I would inform them of the latest rate or promotional offers, and clarify special instructions. The instructions varied between the most straightforward, such as picking up from the back porch, to the most long-winded explanation revealing familial dynamics and conflicts. A customer in her 60s who alternated sending to two presumably grown-up children with children of their own, never failed to instruct me that the box should be delivered on a specific day and time. "Make sure they don't deliver the box to my daughter on a Friday afternoon *ha*," she would repeat over and over "I can only send one box this time and my son usually visits my daughter on Fridays. If he finds out I sent *balikbayan* to her he would feel slighted. I have not filled up *his* box yet." No matter how I explained that a precise day and time of delivery could not be guaranteed, as it always depended on the number of boxes to be distributed in an area, she still insisted on her own exact planning, as though the welfare of her entire family depended on the fixed arrival of that box.

The second task was to plan the route of the pickup. After receiving all requests for the day, I would group them with all previous calls and separate them by the zones that we established for Chicago. The pickup each day rotated among these zones. I pinned on a digital map the addresses where the pickups would be. This was where I would learn again and again how the Filipinos in Chicago were equally ubiquitous and invisible.

As a city, Chicago is a collection of villages only they are called neighborhoods. The South Side has been traditionally identified for black families. A little north of that is Pilsen, home to Latino communities from Mexico, Nicaragua, Costa Rica, El Salvador and South American countries. Puerto Ricans and Cubans have their separate barrios. Then there are the historical neighborhoods for Ukrainians, Czechs, Hungarians, Polish, German, Swedish, Italians, Irish, Jewish, Greeks and more recently, Assyrians, Lithuanians, Slovakians, Latvians, and Armenians. Chinatown has for a long time been a permanent fixture in the southwest side of the city but further up north, separate neighborhoods have sprouted for Japanese, Koreans, Thais, and Vietnamese with a block here and there of businesses by Hmongs, Laotians, and Malaysians. Rogers Park seems to be the preferred areas for the African diaspora from Tanzania, Nigeria, Kenya, Senegal, and Ethiopia. A little bit west of Rogers Park are the communities of Indians, Pakistanis, and Bangladeshis. The islanders of Jamaica and Haiti prefer the suburbs. But there is no Filipino neighborhood.

Based on the 2015 data by Pew Research Center, Chicago held the sixth largest Filipino population in the U.S., after New York, Honolulu, and the Californian cities of Los Angeles,

San Francisco, and San Diego. Within Chicago, Filipinos are the third largest Asian population, after Chinese and Indians. Unlike many communities, the Filipino model of migration in Chicago seems to be assimilation, aiming for absorption into the mainstream, organically or even purposefully defying the establishment of an enclave. But it is also this assimilation that makes Filipinos invisible, secreted between Asians and Latinos, between East and West, and between immigrants and citizens. Because all 140 thousand or so Filipinos in Chicago are everywhere, they are nowhere.

AFTER PLACING ALL ADDRESSES on the map, I would strategize the most efficient route for our drivers. I had to determine their first pickup, which household would be next, and so on, until all the arrangements for a day had been completed. Once the sequence was established, I would calculate the driving time between each house, considering the hour of the day, the flow of the traffic, and amount of time to carry the boxes from house to van. This was the part I had learned to appreciate the most. This was where I gradually discovered the Filipinos in that massive disparate city. Increasingly, I noted which neighborhoods and corners, boulevards and streets, alleys and buildings, apartments and floors they settled in. On the map, my countrymen were pins, like rice grains scattered when a sack is forcibly opened, landing everywhere on the floor, dispersed, without patterns, the same collectively, each house holding its own unique longing.

There were exceptions, naturally. A customer who regularly sent a box every month would give a different address each time she scheduled a pickup. I found out later that she worked as a caregiver, living with her patient for a month before moving to another. There were also two brothers who moved from cousin to cousin, their addresses of pickup changed each time, the address of the destination—their mother's house–remained the same.

At the finalization of the route and schedule, I would call back each customer scheduled for the next pickup to inform them of the estimated time our drivers would drop by their house. This invariably ended up as negotiations, with them requesting for a different time or day and me trying to shut off empathy and consideration. They had work during that time, they would say, and no one was left at home. Most had two or three jobs. They needed another day or two to fill up an additional box to meet new requests from their relatives. They had changed their mind on what to send and were still considering the replacement. Even on the day of pickup, when I had to give them a heads up call that our drivers were only half an hour away, these negotiations could still occur. A customer asked me if they could pick up at the end of the route instead, which would require our team to cross back the entire city, because she was still shopping.

HOMESICKNESS IS AN EXPENSIVE *illness. One fills the absence of relatives and the distance of home with objects that can be bought, driven by dollars earned from two or three jobs, the magnetism of endless shelves in groceries and shops, and the constant prodding on TV that wants are necessities and more, not less, IS more. Eventually, one ends up with three TV sets, two rice cookers, five dozen shoes and boots, three dozen winter coats, and hundreds of discontinued toys and appliances. Each quickly wears out their proxy roles for family back home. Lovingly, they had to be packed and shipped halfway across the world. Thus, a 12-year-old nephew crosses rice paddies wearing a faux-fur-lined winter coat twice oversize. A mother visits next-door neighbors along muddy streets wearing Ann Taylor. The house started accumulating transformers in every corner to plug in 110V DVD players, stereos, and microwave.*

My third task was confirming the delivery of the boxes to the intended family. They initially came as carbon copy pages, with signatures and acknowledgment of condition of the items upon receipt. Eventually, to confirm the delivery, the team in the Philippines decided to take pictures of the *balikbayan* boxes with the recipients. They poured in each month, in thick envelopes with photographs of wide grins, by themselves or with the entire family, standing next a solitary box behind stacks of boxes.

Years later, while working for a technology company in Silicon Valley, I would receive from my former colleagues the last picture of my mother, informing me the boxes I sent were delivered successfully. In the photograph, she sat calmly, her hands on her lap, smiling shyly next to two boxes. It was the smile that I saw first, and often stared at, not knowing–for how could a photograph show that beneath that smile was an illness she was battling, only to lose.

I had that job for only four months. But the map of love and longing in Chicago that I created day after day had been etched for posterity. In my mind, the pins danced in random patterns. They were dances of sadness and homesickness but also of gratitude and remuneration, of material indulgence but also of emotional remedy, of the push for the new land and the pull of the old country.

24

Plastic

DUSTIN DOMINGO

The child-of-immigrant urge to hoard.
Hoard every plastic bag.
Hoard every plastic bucket and box that enters this house.

Sustainable?
Sure.
But there is a deeper story here.
One that tells of the struggle.
The scarcity mindset.
The trauma endured generations over.

Despite that, I am happy.
I am surrounded by love.
I am surrounded by community.

25

August, 2000

SOPHIA EMILLE

That was the year I learned that
summer can be hot and cold at the same time.
At six years old,
this is what I understand to be the American Dream—
opposite origins colliding—
island sand on American soil
cold mornings in a desert valley
mother, breadwinner
father, caretaker
alien child as foreign as the origin
I could never completely identify.

We learned to wear invisibility like a shield,
to move undetected from one dark sunrise to the next.
I learned trust from the backseat of a 1989 Honda Civic,
practiced patience as we drove thousands of miles across
cold dead ends twisting and colliding with
angry words and apologies,
and at the bottom of this valley,
no sunrise would ever find us here.

Where hands hold and pull and scrape and
throw and clench and release
is where we learned to love each other.
Where sweat and tears cut through
skin and memory
is where we taste the ocean water in our blood,
tastes a lot like the salt of American soil.
They stain the fabric of our belonging dark as the
cover of twilight,
dark as the remnants of home now
broken glass lost in the ocean tides.
And we realize
that the backseat sunrises and alienation
were only the beginning.

So, let those deep, broken tides flood the valley
in my lungs now.
In gasping breath and flawed faith,
let these island winds breathe life into
bittersweet American dreams,
fractured origins, dead ends, and all.
Let calloused hands and steady feet
guide us to the mountain peaks,
for we do not belong down here.
We are not this valley.
We are every risk it took to get here.

More than the sum of every mistake and mile marker,
we are red blood stitched across blue waters.
Sunrise to sunset to sky fall, we survive.

We are the place where
island sand and American soil collide.

Thanksgiving Day

ANTHONY TUGADE PABILLANO

November 23, 2000

A plane landed, tossed

    thousands of miles—

from the *pearl of the orient* tarnished

    its luster lost to poverty,

its shape emaciated by hunger,

    its value belittled by homelessness,

but polished, baptized anew in the shores of Corpus Christi.

The Body of Christ

A year I prayed for my father to trace the same path made available to me,

trace the same path I was able to take...

But who knew life would have him follow another instead?

Heart attack.

Just like that. Gone were the prayers I recited every night.

Just like that. Gone is the belief.

Just like that. Gone are tears, dried completely by an eleven-year old kid.

Anthony

'Antonio' was his name—mine,

its mere English counterpart.

THANKSGIVING DAY

Years have passed and not one passes without him passing through my mind.

I ache for all the memories that could have been, but did not,

all the activities a father and son should have shared, but did not.

However, I know he would be grateful for the life I have been able to have here

    since that very first Thanksgiving Day.

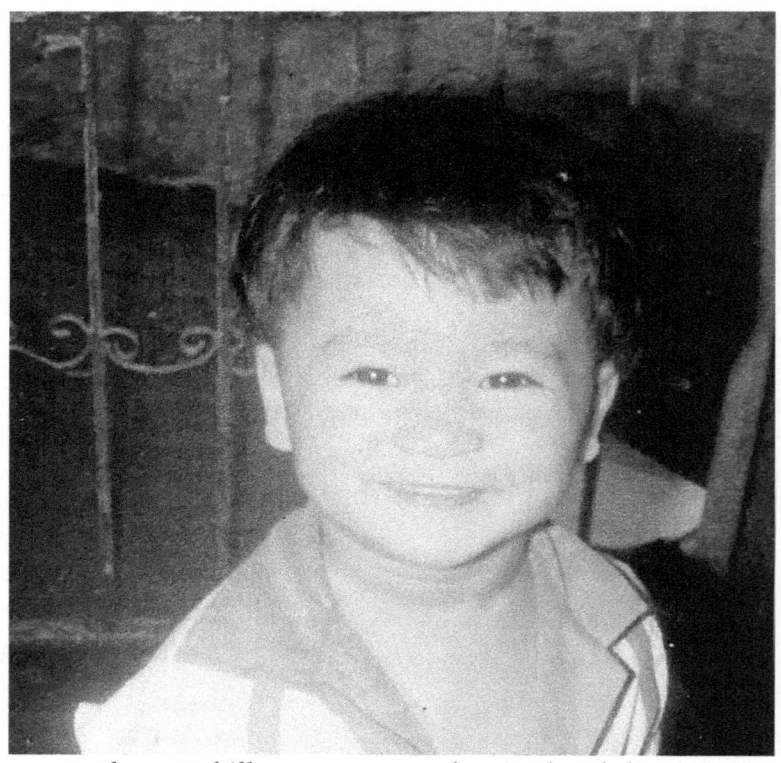
Anthony Pabillano as a young boy in the Philippines

27

A Gaysian Friendsgiving

DUSTIN DOMINGO

It was the first week of November 2011. I came out to Jay just before his 28th birthday. Jay was an old friend of mine whom I'd met through community building work for a Filipino American lifestyle blog called *Bakit Naman*. He was the only man in my immediate circle of friends who I knew to be openly gay.

He stood out as a fresh departure from what I conceptualized as the norm for Filipinos around my age. He was a handsome Filipino man with deep brown skin. His gentleman's haircut had traces of premature salt and pepper strands. He was studying to be a filmmaker. He aspired to be a tour guide and boat skipper for Disneyland's Jungle Cruise. He played in a real life Quidditch league; a sport that was originally invented by JK Rowling for the Harry Potter book series. He was so many things I didn't know I was allowed to be. I was drawn to Jay for that reason. It was important for me to widen my circle of friends to include those who were open about their sexuality so that I could begin to feel closer to who I knew myself to be.

I was 25 years old at this point and I had walked away from yet another breakup. I was depressed. I was lonely. Each of my romantic relationships leading up to this point, be they with men or women, were destined to fail as quickly as they started because at least one of us was in the closet about their sexuality. I was tired of hiding and feeling the pressures of society to live up to expectations that were impossible to reach.

For his birthday, Jay invited me to dinner and beer with him and a few of his friends who were also gay men. We met at a dive bar in Long Beach California. I joined them as an openly fellow gay. Then beer after beer, we exchanged our favorite stories involving Jay's past, present, and future.

One of the guests at the table was JR, a familiar face. I'd met him in passing a few years before at a community event for *Bakit Naman* and he let me know that he'd love to hang out with me more often. After sharing a few beers with my new friends, I knew coming out was the right decision.

At the conclusion of dinner, JR invited me to my first party that was exclusively hosted by a group of Southern California *gaysians*, Gay Asian American young men who were involved in what felt like an elaborate network of good-looking gay men of color worth knowing, friendly or otherwise. I later learned that I could refer to this network of people and associated activities as *the scene*.

"You should come to a *Friendsgiving* potluck, with me and the boys," he said, "It's tomorrow night at 7 p.m. at my buddy's house in Rancho Cucamonga. I'll text you the details. Just bring any food item."

A GAYSIAN FRIENDSGIVING

I was nervous and shy, but I was yearning for gay friends; folks with whom I could relate on a deeper level. "Of course. I'll be there."

He texted me the address the next day and I made quick work of what I had sitting in the dark corners of my kitchen cabinet and refrigerator shelves.

I was living in a Moreno Valley apartment by myself. I found pride in having a space to call my own though I was barely making ends meet; living paycheck to paycheck.

I took a mental inventory of the food items I could find: ½ bag of rice; 1 bag of frozen peas and carrots; 2 cans of spam; 6 eggs; 1 near empty bottle of canola oil; salt; pepper; and 3 packets of soy sauce from the Chinese restaurant down the street.

"Spam fried rice it is!" I cheered to myself.

It was a perfect and simple potluck contribution for a man like me. I liked to tell myself when it came to frugal meal prepping, *why follow a recipe when I can follow my heart.* That's the affirmation I've often used to rationalize my refusal to either measure or purchase ingredients. It's hard to mess up fried rice, and with Spam as the secret ingredient, I thought for certain I'd win over my would-be friends. In this instance, my heart did not fail me. The steam rose from the wok. The rice was crispy, but chewy; slightly browned from the soy sauce. Each cube of Spam was lightly charred, but not burnt. I picked up a spoon and fed myself a small sample; the Spam fried rice was indeed delicious.

I didn't have a smart phone at the time because again, I was living paycheck to paycheck. I had a pay-as-you-go flip phone and with no GPS I needed to find directions to my Rancho Cucamonga destination via MapQuest. Surprise—I also didn't have a printer, so I had to hand write directions onto a scratch piece of paper. All of this delayed my departure; and when I arrived to the Gaysian Friendsgiving, I was nearly an hour late. With a foil covered tray in hand I entered the house. The first thing that hit me was an eruption of boisterous laughter; a signal that the party was well underway. The second thing was the scent. The air was filled with a fusion of chicken enchiladas from the oven, warm cookies on the dinner table, vodka and wine drippings on the floor, and now Spam fried rice, which thankfully stayed warm despite my 45 minute drive.

Almost overwhelming and like a stereotypical house party that young people have in the movies, I had to take a brief pause to mentally prepare myself for the night. The goal was to meet new people and I was there. I had already paid admission with my tray of Spam fried rice. I knew I couldn't turn back.

I set my contribution down next to the other food items and was immediately welcomed by JR. He introduced me to those in my immediate proximity. I was welcomed with open arms and directed to take a shot of vodka before fixing myself a plate. This night and these people led me to some of my closest friends in the years that followed.

Over the years, this friend group has evolved. We've matured. Folks come and go. But that night, I learned that it was far less complicated to connect with other gaysians and that I had the right to be myself even in spaces that were not exclusively queer or Filipino.

Even without the consumption of vodka, tequila, and rum, I knew from that moment that it was okay to be a gay Filipino man. It was okay to simply be me.

28

The Last Feather

RUDY JR. CALERA

Act 1: Scene 1

Mesmerizing eyes, shining brightly.
Red lips, that made me thirsty.
Skin's whiteness, blinding my eyes.
And the posture, that elegant swaying.

Meeting with the creature is truly inevitable.
But, this tingling feeling is unbelievable.
What is this pounding inside my temple?
Is this a miracle and ancient feeling that is unquestionable?

I never thought that I would feel this way.
But, whatever it may—
I hope no one is needed to pay.

Act 1: Scene 2

Welcome to his holy divine land.
Where rules and obligations are in his hands.
Cruelly control the wings of everyone.
But, this mine is probably the worst one.

I conquer and defy the rules in his palm.
Disobeying what he wants from us.
Just for the creature, I saw in a glance.
That I thought were gonna be my last.

Oh! Please! Defying this is hard.
Just be there my one so you can be my love.

Act 1: Scene 3

Every move should synchronize with the others.
So this alien invasion of mine can be concealed.
I confessed everything to this dearest creature.
And in a snap, we're already together.

Against all odds is what we are believing.
Yet, cloudy and dark days are still seeing.
How this feeling can be our everything.
Like a shackle can do, I confined myself in this thing.

Happiness is what we aim for.
But, for some reason, you become a cold and ruthless person.

Act 2: Scene 1

Indeed, trials cannot be denied.
But you know what is unacceptable in this life?
Avert from the adversity and chase for a new time.
A loop where wolves concealed their fangs and established chimes.

Lurking from the dark.
Creature bites this trap.
How foolish you are for falling in this mud.
You jump without testing the land.

In this divine land, where madness is restricted.
Now, these wings are in chaotic aviation.

Act 2: Scene 2

Fly high! Fly high!
Until those wings ignite on reddish fire.
And no one can distinguish it from white.
Just pure dusk and ashes of life.

How cruel this creature is.
I have disobeyed everything since the beginning.
And it turns out that this is the beginning of misery.
Misery in life where those wings can't bear in high.

I thought sharing the same view in the sky is a great idea.
How foolish am I to not consider your eyes when I'm looking above.

Act 2: Scene 3

Where are you now hiding?
I feel blue and alone under the moonlight.
Is this the price of being disobedient?
An unending agony behind this piece of skin?

My feathers are starting to lose.
Where are the hands that I used to hold?
Can someone embrace these wings of mine?
To stop the insecurities hitting me left and right.

But, I guess this creature isn't around anymore.
Is this the real price of being a fool?

Act 3: Scene 1

Now, that I'm on the edge.
Gladly, I found you, but you're wearing something.
A promise ring that I never gave.
And it left me flabbergasted by that scenery.

World seems crushing down and apart.
But, in reality, I'm just broken and shocked.
Now, what is the meaning of this shackle in my hands?
I'm imprisoned yet you roam freely around safe and sound.

Is this the reality that I keep on denying?
Or just my imagination playing with my thinking?

Act 3: Scene 2

This creature seems fine and lovely.
But, what I'm worried about is the blade where it's walking.
Is this what you are really chasing for?
Or it's just the excitement of being together that teased you?

Why? Why did you leave in my wings?
Where are serenity and euphoria lying?
Sorry, for not bringing you the world in one click.
But, I cherished you just how I take care of my wings.

This ending and the creature's situation are familiar in Odin's eyes.
I hope you shouldn't pay the price.

Act 3: Scene 3

Quietly steps back towards my home.
Carrying the ill undying thoughts.
My wings can't fly and drive me home.
Not thinking about society's thoughts.

Now, I'm home.
I'm surprised that everyone knows.
Everyone treated me like a fiend.
For lying and fostering something.

Definitely, this is the price.
Now my wings were taken back from me as a payment.
And now become the fallen angel named—Lucifer.

Epilogue

Flying like a crow in a deserted zone
Where the river of thoughts has a lot of space to devour.
Once an angel who loved a creature
Is now wandering along with his last white feather around.

The End

Image credited to Rudy Jr. Calera

29

Motherland

TIFFANY SLOAN

How surreal it is to meet your mother
when you are fully grown
To see her beauty curated for this first encounter
What an apt comparison:
to equate life to land and the women who tend it.

What do we ask of land when calling her our mother?
What do we ask of women as they hold us?

30

New Moon Peaches

SHERALYNN MAGALLANES

HARVESTING THE FRUIT FROM my grandmother's garden, Picking the last of the summer's harvest of peaches that we'll ever grow in this house.

My grandparents' closure from losing a daughter comes in the form of a new home.

The transition has us taking up more space in this house than we have since my Auntie Jenny passed.

For 7 years my grandparents kept her room completely intact and tended to her grave site every single day.

For 33 years this house had only been home to one family — and every guest with a hearty appetite that found themselves happily stuffed at our dinner table.

For 25 years my Auntie Jenny knew no other house as Home.

NEW MOON PEACHES

And now time seems to be slipping through my fingers as I try to recount every memory we've ever had here, grasping onto as much as I can fit into my head and my heart until we leave.

Every nook, corner and old item is a cherished piece of our family's history.

The more my grandparents let go, the more I want to hold on.

We all grew up here. How could they sell the house?

The answer to my yearning lies in the shrine of my Auntie Jenny's things that sits in the guest room, waiting to be moved.

It's in the empty room upstairs that was once blue with glow in the dark stars on the walls that is now painted white.

It's in the box of baby clothes and a brand new Korean blanket that my Nana was going to give to Auntie Jenny's future daughter, but she gave to me last week.

Closure,
And the chance to write a new chapter—
perhaps their last — in a new space.

They get the keys on Tuesday,
the day after the New Moon.

My grandmother forms community wherever she goes.

The neighbors gather in a joyful farewell full of wine and food.

Between the sips of wine and the conversations with neighbors, I glance up at the house and see a young Jenny

and her niece Lynnie running around the yard,
for sure up to no good.

My eyes refocus to the present and I see the same fierce grandparents with slightly bent backs and a slower pace.

"The peaches aren't good," Nana says.
I take a bite. They're delicious.
I save a few seeds, hoping we can plant peach trees at the new house.

Top left photo: Sheralynn tending to the peach tree; Top right photo: Sheralynn and peach tree; Bottom left photo: Nana; Bottom right photo: Old house

On Performance

TIFFANY SLOAN

Allow me to spit—
To unload the knowledge of a motherland
I may never actually reach
Diasporic mouthpiece unhinged
Breath of ancestral soil, rally cries,
and night crawling activists:
We had to smuggle out the truth

> I've been putting off writing this.
> I've been putting off writing anything.
>
> I'm erasing myself from our narrative.
>
> But whose pain do I feel when
> I leave us in silence?
> Putting pen to paper is an act of defiance
> and I'm slowly unlearning this lesson of refuge in
> quiet.

ON PERFORMANCE

*Who am I to write a movement,
to flow in a medium that doesn't belong to me?*

*Yet who am I to reject her,
to bottle a verse that she might need?*

*Is she not the inspiration,
the motivation, the driving force?
The source and yet the unreachable memory.
The phantom pains of lost time, lost love,
stolen land.*

In truth, there is too much that is yet to be said.

I step to the mic—
Here's a story of an island nation,
and this time we are present at
the center of its narrative. This time,
the islands have made their way to Texas
and it feels like Home.

32

Salamat Houston

GABBIE AQUINO-ADRIATICO

Houston
A NEW PLACE FOR me
filled with growing pains
and also opportunities
lived with uncertainty
but also assurance that this is exactly where I needed to be

Houston
a new place to be
you gave me some of my darkest days
but you also gave me strength, hope, and solitude
where I was homesick
and felt home all at the same time

Houston
the place I became a mommy
where I experienced depleted exhaustion
but also ecstatic excitement to see my baby

SALAMAT HOUSTON

where I struggled to find time for anything
but would do anything for more time with my baby

Salamat Houston
binigyan mo ako nang anak at aso
binigyan mo ako nang bagong kaibigan

Salamat Houston
ikaw ay isang mahirap na teacher
tinuruan mo ako nang maraming lessons
tinuruan mo ako paano magbigay nang mahal when
akala ko hindi ko na kaya
tinuruan mo ako na okay lang kung hindi ko alam

Salamat Houston
tinulungan mo ako
minahal mo ako
at binigyan mo ako nang bagong buhay

Thank You Houston

English Translation

Houston
a new place for me
filled with growing pains
and also opportunities
lived with uncertainty
but also assurance that this is exactly where I needed to be

Houston
a new place to be
you gave me some of my darkest days
but you also gave me strength, hope, and solitude
where I was homesick
and felt home all at the same time

Houston
the place I became a mommy
where I experienced depleted exhaustion
but also ecstatic excitement to see my baby
where I struggled to find time for anything
but would do anything for more time with my baby

Thank you Houston
you gave me a son and dog
you gave me new friends

Thank you Houston
you are a difficult teacher
you taught me many lessons
you taught me how to give love
when I thought I couldn't do it
you taught me that it's okay even if I didn't know

SALAMAT HOUSTON

Thank you Houston
you helped me
you loved me
and you gave me a new life

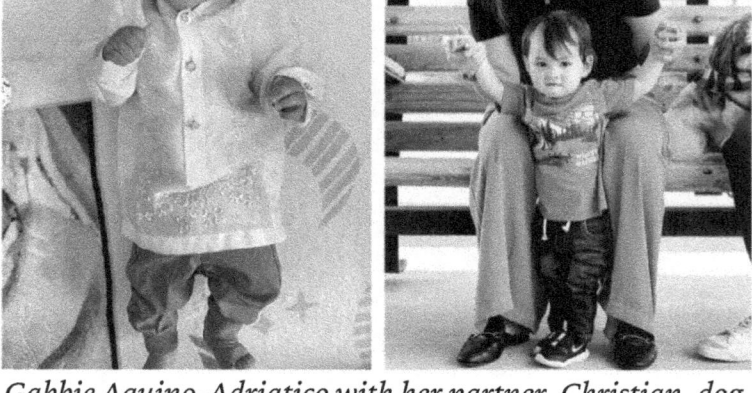

Gabbie Aquino-Adriatico with her partner, Christian, dog, Bentley, and baby, Greyson

33

Uwi Na Tayo

ZOE GAPAYAO

Hinila ko ang damit ng lolo ko. "Uwi na tayo!" ang sabi ko. Nasa kalesa kami sa Intramuros nung nakita ko na malungkot sila lolo at lola. Ang ibig ko sabihin ay "umuwi na tayo sa Bicol" galing sa Maynila, kaso naroon pala kami dahil sasakay ako ng eroplano patungo sa aming bagong bansa. Ito ang aking huling alaala bago ako umalis ng Pilipinas.

Kahit ilang buwan na kami sa EU, madalas ni papa pina-alala sa akin na, "Huwag mo kalimutan kung saan naroon ang iyong tahanan." Maraming taon na ang nakalipas, at hindi ko ito nakalimutan.

Pagkatapos ng ilang taon, nakabalik ako sa aking inang-bayan; pareho pa rin ang pagmamahal ko dito. Maganda pa rin ang kanyang mga kagubatan at karagatan, pero naghihirap katulad ng taong bayan. Noong nakuha ko ang aking dalawang pagkamamamayan, ako ay mas nakiramay sa aking inang bayan. Ang pangangalaga at pagprotekta ng kalikasan ng Pilipinas ay naging isa sa pinakamahalagang dahilan ng pagbalik ko sa aking tahanan.

Let's Go Home

English Translation

I tugged at my *lolo's* clothes. "Let's go home!" I said. We were in the carriage in Intramuros when I saw my grandparents' sadness. What I meant was, "Let's go home to Bicol" from Manila, where instead I would be boarding a plane to our new country. This is my last memory before I left the Philippines.

Even though we had been in the United States for a few months, my papa often reminded me, "Don't forget where your home is." Many years have passed, and I have never forgotten it.

After several years, I was able to return to my motherland; my love for her has not waned. Still her forests and oceans are beautiful, but suffering like her people. When I became a dual citizen, I sympathized more with my motherland. I return home to care for and protect the natural resources of the Philippines.

Ilawod with Family

The Land Loves Us Back

SHERALYNN MAGALLANES

A poem inspired by artwork by Molly Costello

I dream of a garden where the roots of the fruits & vegetables are as diverse as the roots of the people that tend to it

Where the harvest is as rich and abundant as the souls and minds of those who pick and water it

Where the children who come to participate learn the value not only in dedication & consistency but also patience, careful attention, and tender care

Where the adults who come to help are healed from their pain through community and love

Where we feed the land and it feeds us back;
Where we love the land and it loves us back

Where we work for and with each other and everybody eats

Where the ways of sustainability & community are re-learned from the ways of our respective ancestors who lived off the land intimately and knew how efficient, harmonious, and fruitful we can be as one life force before western colonization exploited us all

A place where we can tune back into our Mother Earth and feel the mothers of our grandmothers, and their mothers, through Her

A place where we can feed not only our own children, but all children

And re-teach them the true histories
of their respective peoples,
talk in our native tongues,
dance our traditional dances,
adorn ourselves rightfully so,
and revel in each other and all that life has to offer

A place where our mere existence is the strongest form of our resistance

Where our rest is sacred
Our joy a birthright
Our inherent abundance expressed and guaranteed
Because although we have been displaced
Exploited, severed, disconnected, and spread out

We are still here
We will always find each other
And we always will be

Reflection Questions

AFTER READING THE BOOK or a couple of chapters, here are some reflection questions for you to think about. You can discuss these questions in a a group—with friends and family, or in a class or book club. You can also write your thoughts in your journal, or feel free to share them with Dr. Pinky and Kuwento Co. via email info@kuwentoco.com or social media @KuwentoCo .

1. Which stories and poems resonated with you the most? Why?

2. How similar or different are the *kuwentos* about growing up with your own experiences?

3. Have you ever moved to a new country and place? What was it like?

4. What is your experience around the concept of home and family?

5. How has the role of women, mothers, and grandmothers impacted your life?

6. Several contributing authors shared and grappled with their intersecting identities, such as culture, ethnicity, nationality, immigration status, generation, gender, sexual orientation, and socioeconomic status. What are your intersections of identity and how do they shape your life?

7. In what ways do your experiences differ or relate to contributing author's dreams, fears, accomplishments, and obstacles?

8. How do you process loss—albeit loss of self, a loved one, or through COVID-19?

9. What does community mean to you? What does it mean to give back? How can you and others transform a community?

10. How does this book spotlight the Filipina/x/o diaspora? What did you learn about the lives and experiences of Filipinas/xs/os in this anthology?

11. If you were to write your own chapter for *The Kuwento Book*, what would you write and why?

12. If you could ask the editor and/or contributing authors any question(s), what would it be?

Acknowledgements

Kuwento Co. would like to acknowledge and thank every contributing author who bravely shared their *kuwentos*: Al Aguilar, Anthony Tugade Pabillano, Chezka Laddaran, Christy Panis Poisot, Cybil Joy Pallugna-Saenz, Dustin Domingo, Florencio Guinhawa, G. Chris Villanasco, Gabbie Aquino-Adriatico, Genesis Lingling, Holly Lim, Jacob Magallanes, Jay Menes, Jermuel P. Manarin, Krystelle Robeniol, Krystle Tugadi, Marie Salazar, Noureliza Montifar, Royal Sumikat, Rudy Jr. Calera, Sheralynn Magallanes, Sophia Emille, Tiffany Sloan, Trisha Morales, Victor Barnuevo Velasco, and Zoe Gapayao.

Special thank you to Jenah Maravilla for the heartfelt foreword.

About the Contributing Authors

Contributing Authors are listed in alphabetical order by first name.

AL AGUILAR *is a creative person struggling to uncork his creativity. Writing poems has offered therapeutic comfort and ambitious exploration in times of isolation or curiosity. Al was interested in writing poetry after completing a poetry assignment for a high school English class—his teacher liked his poem and encouraged him to write more. In college, Al*

took an Intro to Poetry class and got introduced to poets like William Blake, Emily Dickinson, and T.S. Eliot; these poets motivated him to work more on the craft of writing poems. He still writes to this day, though, not as much as he used to, but he still gets excited when he is able to get words on a page and arrange their relationship to each other like a puzzle.

ANTHONY TUGADE PABILLANO *(he/siya) is a Houston-based visual artist who immigrated from the Philippines. As an artist, he focuses on portraiture based on realism, rooted on his desire to explore various aspects of the human condition and experience, from ideas relating to self and identity, to topics about diversity. His current*

artistic pursuit is to visually celebrate the diversity and the individual stories of the people he meets whose walks of life all led to the multiculturally-, multinationally-, and multi-ethnically-rich city of Houston, Texas—the place he calls home.

CHEZKA LADDARAN—*you can call her Chez. She accomplished her Bachelor's degree in Psychology and is an advocate of mental health. When the world is filled with so much pain and fear, writing has been Chezka's escape. When there's so many things left unsaid, she uses her pen and paper to express her emotions. Though she is in the process of learning in the field of writing, she hopes that through her words, she can make an impact on others.*

ABOUT THE CONTRIBUTING AUTHORS

CHRISTY PANIS POISOT *has worked for Shell USA Inc. for twenty-five years. She currently works as an Information Digital Technical Advisor for Subsurface & Wells with a deep background in Information Risk Management, Cybersecurity, Downstream Manufacturing, HR IT operations, project management, and strategy and planning. As a champion for diversity, she was President of Shell's US Women's Group WAVE (Women Adding*

Value Everywhere). In 2016, she was recognized by Shell Oil Company with the "They Serve with Honor" award. The event was hosted by the OCA-Asian Pacific American Advocates of Greater Houston (OCA-GH) to ensure that Asian Americans are recognized in the community by businesses and corporations. Her 2016 accomplishment as Board member of The Filipino Veterans Recognition and Education Project was the passage of a bill through Congress to recognize WWII Filipino Veterans with the Congressional Gold Medal. Christy serves the Filipino community as the National Vice President of the Filipino American National Historical Society (FANHS). In 2018, she co-authored and published the book "Filipinos in Houston" during her tenure as the FANHS-Houston Chapter President.

CYBIL JOY PALLUGNA-SAENZ *is a second-generation Filipinx. She is a self-taught, multidisciplinary artist, community leader, mystical practitioner, and storyteller. She is a daughter of Filipino immigrants from the island of Luzon (Quezon) and ancestral lineage from the island of Mindanao. Cybil traces her familial origins in the occupied and unceded land of the Sana, Atakapa-Ishak, Akokisa, and Karankawa people's territory (Houston, Texas) as far back as the 1980s.*

She is a humble culture bearer and descendent of a barangay captain, pharmacist, seamstress, and tailor. Cybil creates narrative and documentary short films, records digital media to document Fil-Am community histories, and explores fiber art through macrame. Cybil's narrative is influenced by her exploration of precolonial history in the Philippines and how she processes her existence and identity impacted by colonization.

DUSTIN DOMINGO, *Ed.D. is an educator who challenges conceptualizations of professionalism and leadership. He advocates for the representation and empowerment of minorities in spaces from the workplace to social media. Outside of his 10+ years in education, Dustin is a musician and podcaster. With Filosophy, an acappella group composed of Asian American singers, Dustin is a regular performer with credits at the Festival of Philippine Arts & Culture, Knott's Berry Farm, Disney's California Adventure, and Downtown Disney. Dustin also co-hosts MeSearch, a podcast which*

features critical conversations with friends and trailblazers in the Filipino community.

ABOUT THE CONTRIBUTING AUTHORS

A native of Bauan, Batangas, **FLORENCIO "FLOR" C. GUINHAWA** *is the 3rd son to Gregorio and Esperdiona Guinhawa. Flor moved to Pasay City in 1952, where he finished elementary and secondary education. He graduated with a degree of BSChE from Mapua Institute of Technology in 1970. Flor was formerly married to Elizabeth Garcia*

with whom he has 3 children Ricky, Willette, and Willie and a stepdaughter Aileen. He now has 4 grandchildren. His family immigrated to the United States in 1973. Flor and his sons moved to Houston in 1979 where he is still a resident. Flor worked mainly in the oil and gas field as a Control Systems Design Engineer Supervisor with the longest tenure at Bechtel Corporation for over 39 years. As an active member of the Fil-Am Houston community, Flor was a founding member of Filipino American Council of Southern Texas (FACOST) in 1993 and Philippine American Chamber of Commerce Texas (PACCTX) in 2007. His hobbies are photography, dabbling in crossword puzzles, and reading books of David Baldacci, John Grisham, and David Brown to name a few.

ABOUT THE CONTRIBUTING AUTHORS

G. CHRIS VILLANASCO *is an English Professor at Lone Star College, teaching Rhetoric and Composition and Literature. She has also enjoyed acting in a few of the college theatre productions. She was born in the Philippines and immigrated to the U.S. when she was two years old, growing up in Virginia. She lives in Southeast Texas with her husband and calls her immediate family members every week and*

regularly texts her cousins all over the world. Losing Lola is her first submission of a memoir for publication.

ABOUT THE CONTRIBUTING AUTHORS

GABBIE AQUINO-ADRIATICO *is a doctoral candidate, social work researcher, educator, and lifelong learner. Her work is guided by postcolonial thought, intersectionality, and culturally embedded theories. Gabbie draws her strength from her lolos and lolas whose roots are from Pagsanjan, Laguna, and Teacher's Village, Quezon City. Gabbie was*

raised in Southern California but currently attends school in Houston. As a first-generation college and graduate student, she would not be here if it weren't for her family, sister circles, and community. Gabbie believes that kuwentos are generational wisdom that can heal and transform the world. Gabbie dedicates her kuwentos to her baby, Greyson, furbaby, Bentley, and partner, Christian.

GENESIS SORIANO LINGLING *is from Purok 3 Brgy. Caglanipao Sur, Calbayog City, Samar, Philippines. He is the son of Michael Lingling and Angelina Lingling. Genesis came from a poor family who really valued education since they believe that it is one of the greatest treasures an individual could achieve. He is a proud graduate of Caglanipao*

Sur Elem. School, San Isidro National High School, and Northwest Samar State University. He is a certified scholar of the ESGP-PA, one of the scholarship programs sponsored by the Government under 4P's for 4 years. Genesis is a current scholar of the SEOMEO Innotech-NEAP Program by the Department of Education. Currently, he is a Public School Teacher teaching at Tabawan Integrated School.

HOLLY LIM *is the CEO and founder of Holly Lim Strategies, where she is a strategic activator of leadership for BIPOC leaders and teams. She uses racial-equity and healing justice frameworks, grassroots organizing strategies, and holistic approaches to guide leaders toward solutions. She has an MA in Asian American studies and a BA in*

political science/law & society. Her graduate research was on Asian American women political leadership stories and pathways. She was a program director for a leadership development program, where she hosted First Lady Michelle Obama for a leadership conversation. Connect with Holly on www.HollyLimStrategies.com

ABOUT THE CONTRIBUTING AUTHORS

JACOB MAGALLANES *is a high school student attending La Salle College Preparatory, who lives in Pasadena, CA. One of his hobbies is writing; he writes to create worlds he can only dream about and share his experiences with the world. When he was ten years old, he wrote his first novel, "Lumpy Trumpy"—a short fiction about twin siblings trying to stop Donald Trump from running for presidency. Besides writing, he also loves bodybuilding, baseball, and motorsports. In particular, he has been racing cars since he was five years old with the support of his mom and dad. Jacob plans to major*

in either Mechanical Engineering or Physical Therapy while pursuing an opportunity to maintain his racing career.

JAY MENES *is a multi-talented artist who has been working as a host, actor, assistant director, facilitator, literacy advocate, oral storyteller, entrepreneur, and adventurer. He is the prime mover in promoting the Art of Oral Storytelling through Storyhouse Philippines since March 2011. He has performed at festivals in Hawaii & California*

(U.S.A.), Singapore, Morocco, Sharjah (U.A.E.), and Iran. Jay is the winner of the 17th Iran International Storytelling Festival. He is a member of the Federation of Asian Storytellers (FEAST) and of NCCA- National Committee on Dramatic Arts. Lastly, he is the first Filipino member of the International Storytelling Network Red Internacional de Cuentacuentos. Connect with Jay on https://www.facebook.com/storyhousephilippines/

JENAH MARAVILLA *(she/her) may be an organizer and activist, but has always been a writer. An Alumnus of both Texas A&M University and Texas Tech Health for B.S. in Nursing, Maravilla permanently pivoted away from healthcare when co-authoring Filipinos in Houston with Christy Poisot. Alongside being the founding Secretary of*

UniPro Texas and participating in both FANHS Houston and Filipinx Artists of Houston, she became inspired by our storytellers to show up in historically exclusive spaces. All of Maravilla's work centers around honoring those that came before, empowering those present, and shifting the conversation to radical vulnerability. Read more about Jenah on https://jnhm.carrd.co/

ABOUT THE CONTRIBUTING AUTHORS

JERMUEL P. MANARIN *was born in Cavite City. He is an Associate Research Writer at Jpapers Philippines and a registered National Book Development Board author. He graduated Cum Laude with a Bachelor of Arts in English Language Studies in August 2022. Throughout college, he was a consistent awardee of the Dean's and President's Lists. He always loved writing ever since he was little. It's always been a way for him to escape, to create his worlds*

and characters. He is also very creative and loves to see his creations come to life.

KRYSTELLE ROBENIOL *is a lifelong learner and has a passion for education, service, outreach, and conflict resolution. She received her BA in Sociology, MA in Organizational Psychology, and graduate certificate in Mind, Brain, and Teaching. She is a learning coach, client success manager, professional mediator, a writer, dog mama*

to two pups and soon-to-be mama to a new human being in summer 2023. She lives in Anaheim, CA with her loving and wonderful husband, JB.

KRYSTLE TUGADI *is an actor, singer, and writer based out of Los Angeles, California. She received her M.F.A. in Acting at California Institute of the Arts and her B.A. in Theatre at California State University, Dominguez Hills. Krystle is also a singer-songwriter and has written, composed, and produced her own album entitled, Time, which debuted in 2011. She has also teamed up with one of her closest pals, Dustin Domingo, to produce the podcast called "MeSearch". The podcast reclaims the academic term that has historically been viewed in a negative light to celebrate and highlight*

the Filipino/x/a-American experience and the community's leaders.

ABOUT THE CONTRIBUTING AUTHORS

MARIE SALAZAR *practiced Dentistry in the Philippines for 25 years, owning multiple dental clinics and diagnostic centers. Marie enjoys her time as a Registered Orthodontic assistant while working on her license to practice Dentistry here in the U.S. She is a proud mother of two grown-up daughters. She loves to travel, and connect and learn from*

diverse cultures. Marie spends her free time in the countryside close to nature, finding solitude and peace.

ABOUT THE CONTRIBUTING AUTHORS

NOURELIZA MONTIFAR *is the second generation in her family to grow up in the U.S. She was born to a Filipino mom and Moroccan dad. She grew up in New York City and currently resides in Houston, TX. Noureliza has always been interested in natural health and even more so since her mom was diagnosed with dementia. She is a big advocate for*

helping and educating the Filipino community about health and wellness. Noureliza is one of the leaders in the Houston Filipino Community, leading as the President of Filipino Young Professionals in Houston and helping as a member of Filipino American National Historical Society- Houston, Texas (FANHS-HTX). She is a mom of three awesome children. She loves to compete in races such as marathons and triathlons. Noureliza loves to connect with people and help others. Connect with her on instagram @SuperMom_Nour

ABOUT THE CONTRIBUTING AUTHORS

*Born in the Philippines and currently residing in Houston, Texas — multi-city muralist and painter, **ROYAL SUMIKAT**, is a dynamic human and a futuristic artist. She works with spray paint, gouache, acrylic paints, markers, and Procreate. Royal's work is informed by her experiences as an immigrant, community organizer, and priestess— taking inspiration from the spaces afforded by these different identities. Storytelling and mythology is prevalent in her work as she aims to strengthen the connection she has with her ancestors.*

ABOUT THE CONTRIBUTING AUTHORS 217

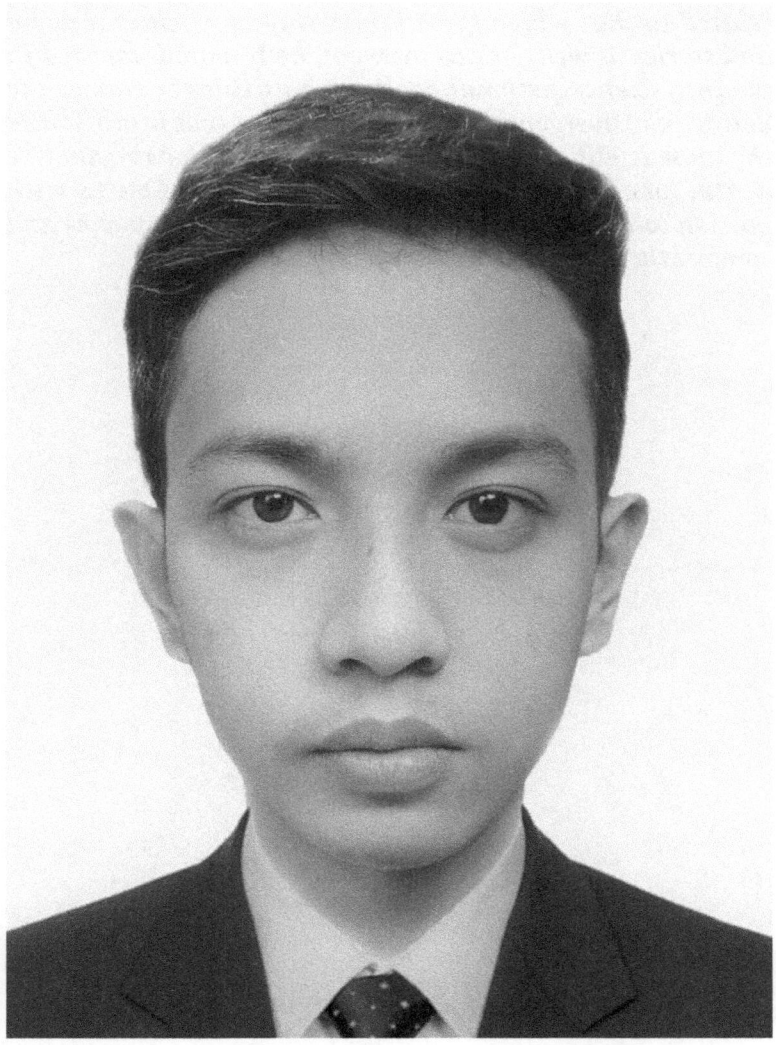

RUDY JR. CRUZ CALERA *resides in Quezon City and is studying Business Administration major in Human Resource Management at Polytechnic University of the Philippines. He uses Scriveners as his pen name since this is the name of the group he created on social media where they offer free poems and stories to people. Since grade school, one of his hobbies is*

reading and writing. He would read stories from textbooks in school and even at the library, then he will create something related to that which gives him a way to produce a poem and stories as well. At this moment, he is more interested in reading science-fictional books such as Hunger Games the Series and Divergent the Series. The writer that inspired him the most is Edgar Allan Poe, who is known for themes like death, loss of love, and regret. As a writer, he burns with passion to do more, and to reach people through poems and comfort them with his words and phrases.

SHERALYNN MAGALLANES *(she/her) is the proud daughter of a single mother, the granddaughter of immigrants from the Philippines and Korea, and has an estranged white grandfather. As a mixed race Filipina, generational healing is her North Star, and writing is one of her forms of medicine. In addition to being a writer, Sheralynn is a mental health and wellness professional in higher education with a background in communication and*

diversity, equity, and inclusion. Her social change roles are Visionary, Weaver, Caregiver, and Healer. She is a woman of the Bay Area, born and raised.

SOPHIA EMILLE *is a Filipino writer and performance poet from Houston, Texas. The daughter of Filipino immigrants, her work strives to examine the values and conflicts that immigrant life places on her heritage, and the many facets of being both an American and a foreigner. She has performed as a feature poet for Galveston's Coast2Soul poetry open mic; the Houston Public Poetry 2019 Summer and Winter Reading series; Houston's Bayouth Teen Slam; and as part of*

the HTX Slam team in San Antonio's 2nd Verse poetry open mic. She is a part-time student and caregiver currently living in Houston.

ABOUT THE CONTRIBUTING AUTHORS 223

TIFFANY SLOAN *is a spoken word artist who writes to understand her position as a biracial Filipina in the context of the Philippine diaspora. Her work threads her experiences with transnational activism, community organizing, and personal growth into lyrical narratives of self and struggle.*

In all things, Tiffany hopes to steward the voices of her community and center their calls of liberation.

TRISHA MORALES *(she/her) is a Filipina-American Creative Director based in Houston, Texas and an alumnus from Texas A&M University with a B.S. in Electronic Systems Engineering. She currently leads interdisciplinary teams to develop brand strategies and digital media campaigns for up and coming brands, established companies, and non-profits.*

Morales was a former Marketing Director for UniPro Texas as well as part of the Co-Founding Team, a member of FANHS Houston, FxAH, and Impact Hub. With community she hopes to build spaces that empower folks to strengthen their collaborative work and create a deeply caring, inclusive, and equitable world.

VICTOR BARNUEVO VELASCO *lives in Miami since 2010, after 10 years of living in Chicago. He works as an I.T. consultant. His fiction and poetry have appeared in Philippines Graphic, the Cultural Center of the Philippines literary journal Ani, Bicol Journal of Literature, Santelmo, Graphic Reader, softblow, Impossible Archetype, TLDTD,*

Migozine, and other fine journals. He also curates art shows. Currently, his photo exhibit on Philippine Martial Law is touring U.S. cities for a year.

ABOUT THE CONTRIBUTING AUTHORS

ZOE GAPAYAO *is a 1.5 generation Filipina-American who was born in Bicol (Sorsogon) and has roots in Ilocos (Nueva Ecija), Mindanao (Iligan and Cotabato), and Negros (Dumaguete). Zoe works in the environmental and social justice fields with focuses in community engagement and digital media. Zoe serves as the Oral History Chair for*

the Houston chapter of the Filipino American National Historical Society and strives to deepen connections both in the homeland and the diaspora.

About the Editor

DR. PAT LINDSAY "PINKY" C. CATALLA-BUSCAINO

PAT LINDSAY C. CATALLA-BUSCAINO, Ed.D. *(she/her)*, known as **Dr. Pinky**, is the Founder and CEO of Kuwento Co. LLC, a woman-and BIPOC-owned publishing company. She is passionate about helping people write, share, tell, and publish their life stories, kuwentos. She is driven to create the largest collection of *kuwentos* in the world so that BIPOC and marginalized communities, such as the Filipino community, will

ABOUT THE EDITOR

always have a voice, be remembered, honored, and represented by their own accord.

Dr. Pinky is a scholar-activist, community leader, public speaker, and educator. She has 2 decades of combined experience in higher education and grass-roots community organizing for the Asian American Pacific Islander community and the Filipino American community. Dr. Pinky is the current President of Filipino American National Historical Society-Houston, Texas Chapter (FANHS-HTX) and one of the founding chapter charter members since 2015. She is a proud alumna of the University of California, Riverside, University of Houston, and Sam Houston State University.

As an independent and boutique publisher, she debuted her publishing company with 6 author's life story, heirloom books: *Chasing A Dream, The Oscar Tree, Living An Inspired Life: Dula Ng Aking Buhay, Salaysay Ng Aking Buhay: The Story of My Life, The Roots, and Bakas Ng Aking Buhay: The Footprints of My Life. The Kuwento Book: An Anthology of Filipino Stories + Poems* is the first anthology of Kuwento Co. and the premiere book of The Kuwento Book Anthology Series. For more information about Kuwento Co., visit www.KuwentoCo.com or email Dr. Pinky at info@kuwentoco.com

What is your *kuwento*?

This question is the basis of every book. Everyone has life stories, but few people write them down and turn it into a book because people do not know where to begin or how to start. The time to start is now!

Kuwento Co. is a writing, storytelling, and publishing company specializing in empowering BIPOC communities, especially Filipina/x/o people to write, tell, share, and publish their life stories, *kuwentos*.

If you have a dream of creating books based on your life stories, Kuwento Co. will help you step-by-step to become the author of your own *kuwentos* so you can express your authentic self, be heard, inspire others, and pass down your legacy to the next generation.

Here are testimonies about Kuwento Co. and the Founder + CEO, Dr. Pat Lindsay "Pinky" C. Catalla-Buscaino:

"Special thanks to Dr. Pinky who initiated this Kuwento Co, my life story, for the purpose of knowing our heritage for the next generations to come."-O.C.

Special thanks to Kuwento Co. and Dr. Pinky for giving me the chance to gather all my thoughts and legacies of my life stories."-P.C.

"My deepest gratitude to Kuwento Co. and Dr. Pinky for her unwavering support, her persistent guidance and encouragement, without which I will never finish my KUWENTO." -M.M.

"I can never thank enough Kuwento Co. and Dr. Pinky for encouraging me to write. She gave me motivation at a time when my confidence and personal esteem were at low points because of my advanced age...Dr. Pinky laid down the rules in the form of motivational questionnaires. I followed the rules and steps. My writing becomes alive with the events of the past and the present about my parents and siblings, my children and grandchildren for whom my writing is solely dedicated."-E.N.

"Thank you to Kuwento Co. and Dr. Pat Lindsay Carijutan Catalla Buscaino for this writing. It would not have been possible without your advice and guidance. Without you, I could not have imagined myself to write and learn to put my writing into manageable chunks and focus on producing quality materials to create a publishable, final draft of my work of which I can be proud. Thank you for giving me a chance to write about my sad life story, but a triumph in the end that tells me anything is possible if you try hard to make it happen." -L.P.

Perhaps you may not be ready for a whole book? You can always become a contributing author in the The Kuwento Book Anthology series and submit a story or poem based on your life.

Visit **www.KuwentoCo.com** for more information on how you can grow your own kuwento collection.

www.ingramcontent.com/pod-product-compliance
Lightning Source LLC
Chambersburg PA
CBHW032222080426
42735CB00008B/681